HIT
YOUR
POTENTIAL

Mastering the Ted Williams Approach

Steve Ferroli

with a Foreword by Ted Williams

MP
MASTERS PRESS

NTC/Contemporary Publishing Group

A Masters Press book

Published by Contemporary Books

A division of NTC/Contemporary Publishing Group, Inc.

4255 West Touhy Avenue, Lincolnwood (Chicago), Illinois 60646-1975 U.S.A.

Printed and bound in the United States of America.

International Standard Book Number: 1-57028-183-1

10   9   8   7   6   5   4   3   2   1

Library of Congress Cataloging-in-Publication Data

Ferroli, Stephen J.
Hit your potential : mastering the Ted Williams approach /
Stephen J. Ferroli ; with foreword by Ted Williams

        p.   cm.

   Rev. ed. of : Disciple of a master. c1987

   ISBN 1-57028-183-1

   1. Batting (Baseball) 2. Williams, Ted, 1918-   .

   I. Ferroli, Stephen J. Disciple of a master.

   II. Title.

GV869.F47   1998   98-10406

796.357'26--dc21   CIP

To Ted, and all the young baseball players of America, who dream, as I did, of becoming great hitters. May this too help them on their way...

Credits:

Cover Graphics courtesy Steve Ferroli
Cover Design by Phil Velikan
Inside Photos by Charles Bradford
Graphic Assistance by Jason Higgley, Christina Smith
and Terry Varvel
Original Diagrams by Ken Dickinson
Edited by Chad Woolums

ACKNOWLEDGMENTS

Thanks go out to the following:

The All Dorchester Sports League

Charles Bradford

Bridgewater State College

Jack Edwards

MB and Jim Edwards

Adam Frattasio

The John Curtis Free Library

Earl Mathewson

Jane Mathewson

Donna Mazzamurro

Bill Nowlin

Pembroke Recreation

Warren Place

Ted Williams

John Henry Williams

Greg Wood

Special thanks to:

Ted Williams Family Enterprises, Ltd.

And the people at Masters Press:

Tom Bast (Publisher)

Tom Doherty (Sales & Marketing Manager)

Holly Kondras (Senior Editor)

Ken Samelson (Senior Editor)

Chad Woolums (Editor)

CONTENTS

F O R E W O R D

I've been talking about this guy for fifteen years! Still, he doesn't get the attention he deserves because he didn't play baseball professionally. It's really not fair. The way I see it, hitting a baseball and teaching someone to hit a baseball are two different things. And I'll tell you what — Steve Ferroli can teach it every bit as good as I could hit it!

I took the game of baseball quite seriously and looking back I guess I did alright. But when age started kicking me in the pants, I got to thinking more and more about kids — kids and baseball. I began to think about coaching and just how important quality coaching is. Then I thought boy, who out there is going to be able to talk hitting and get it right? Who has the knowledge to answer the big league questions and the heart to put it on the line for the kids? I was describing Steve Ferroli.

How good is he, you may ask? Well, I'll give you some numbers... There are millions of kids between the ages of 8-12 years old playing baseball all around the world. They have been playing in organized youth leagues in our country since 1939. But, they have been playing a game that is out of scale considering their size and age! Some of the dimensions were simply not scaled down correctly to account for the smaller bodies of these players. As a result, the game is affected — the fun, the interest! When you read Chapter Nine of this book, The Ted Williams League, consider how many hundreds of thousands of coaches, umpires and parents have had this mistake right under their noses but couldn't see it. For over half a century no one saw it — except Steve Ferroli.

It is my sincere hope that he stays in baseball and teaches hitting forever. That's because among all the players, coaches, students, teachers, professors... *anybody* with whom I've ever talked hitting, Steve Ferroli knows more about my principles of hitting than anyone I've ever known.

I N T R O D U C T I O N

Ted Williams always made time for kids. The stories are legendary. He actively promoted children's cancer research through the Jimmy Fund. He would always take a young prospect aside for a half-hour of personal instruction, even one from an opposing team. He would often stop by the roadside to chat when he came across a pickup game.

Steve Ferroli is a lot like this. He was personally selected by Ted Williams to carry on Ted's instructional legacy. Now he spends all his time thinking, not only about hitting, but about baseball in general and how players of different ages can better enjoy the game.

Steve was twenty-one when he first met Ted Williams. He had just begun as a counselor at the former Ted Williams Baseball Camp in Lakeville, Massachusetts. At a camp staff meeting with the topic of work assignments high on the agenda, camp director Earl Mathewson asked, "Does anyone want the little league batting cage?" As Steve recalls, "I shot my hand up hoping to beat everyone else only to find a room full of chuckling. Little did I know that the little league batting cage had come to be recognized as one of the most trying jobs in the camp and no one wanted it. To a physical education major and a young hitter, it was a job where the single hardest skill in sport would be taught to the most important person."

At Ted Williams Camp the number one rule was that camp was "for the camper." Nicknamed the "Pied Piper" by coach Mathewson, Steve Ferroli soon found that he could not go anywhere on camp grounds without ten to thirty kids following him. He had impressed the most important "person" in camp, each individual kid. Ted Williams was also impressed with Steve's knowledge and enthusiasm. Recently Ted recalled, "He started asking me questions and in a year knew as much about what I had said as I did myself. He logged it all! Hell, to talk to him today, you'd think you were talking to me. Anybody could ask him a question and he'd answer it just like I would. And he knows a *ton* about hitting."

Russell Hubbard, a journalist and former hitting student remarks, "Steve Ferroli could teach both a major leaguer and a little fat kid on the corner and bring them both to their potential."

Steve says, "I teach all hitters from eight years old to forty. The young ones take patience and the old ones take time. None of them are easy. The sixteen-and-under kids are the most important to me because they represent the majority of baseball players and the future of the sport. In Japan, the pro teams take the best coaches and put them at the lower levels which makes a great deal of sense to me."

You can feel Steve's love for coaching immediately and it doesn't take much to get him all wound up and "talking hitting." Parents whose kids have worked with Steve overflow with compliments about his dedication and what his efforts have meant to the growth of their children, not just as hitters or ball players but as maturing youngsters.

"Baseball is life," the T-shirt slogan reads. Steve Ferroli, in urging players to *"hit your potential,"* clearly keeps larger and loftier goals in mind. He and Ted both want the Ted Williams Baseball League to help build the whole person, not just the ball player. "That's the thing about working with kids," Steve says. "If I work with a slumping big leaguer, what do I accomplish? I make some money — in a year, who cares? But to educate a kid, to prolong or enrich his relationship with baseball, now I've done much more than coach. I've "big-brothered" him! As far as I'm concerned, baseball — in its pace and design — is a dress rehearsal of Amercan life in disguise. How many good dress rehearsals does a kid get before his show begins?"

Bill Nowlin

Bill Nowlin, co-founder of Rounder Records, is a life long Ted Williams fan. He is co-author with Jim Prime of Ted Williams: A Tribute *and contributed the Afterword to* Ted Williams' Hit List *by Ted Williams and Jim Prime (both published by Masters Press). Having had the opportunity to see the Ted Williams League principles tested and having witnessed first-hand Steve Ferroli's work with players, Bill has become a convinced supporter.*

HIT YOUR POTENTIAL

Ted Williams: A Lost Model Of Execution

Looking back, it's kind of funny because when I was in grade school the name "Ted Williams" was an aggravation to me. His endorsement of several Sears & Roebuck sporting products put his autograph on what seemed to be everything — bats, gloves, weights, tents, fishing rods — everything! In Sears his name was almost as famous as the little "r" with the circle around it. But couple that kind of autograph exposure with stories from my grandmother about how *"that Williams"* had disgraced baseball by spitting and swearing at those who loved him... and in no time at all I was a kid who had developed a *"williams smilliams"* attitude.

It didn't seem long before my personal quest in hitting led me to the top floor of the John Curtis Free Library in my hometown of

FIG 1-1. *Somewhere between the pages of Ted Williams' The Science of Hitting I fell in love with the challenge and details involved in hitting a baseball.*

Hanover, Massachusetts. It was there I stood as a high school ballplayer — all heart, dreams and desire — and it was there that it all started. Not only did I begin to pay a long string of overdue notices on *The Science of Hitting*, a 97-page classic written by, of all people, Ted Williams, but I also began an endless study of the hardest single act in the sporting world — hitting a baseball. Much like the Atlantic Salmon, I was hooked...

I think everyone gets their calling, and I heard mine when I realized how little the game of baseball knew about hitting years after Williams' book. Though you probably don't realize it, hitters today are far below their potential; and I'm talking from professional baseball right down the line. The quality of the teaching and study of this skill has declined along with its statistics. As a result, hitters today don't know what to do, when to do it, or why to do it. And so, each spring illogical instruction continues to be fed to millions of young hitters from positions of trust, respect and authority.

While my ultimate goal is to help solve the problems in hitting today, I know that goal can only be reached after "the hitting world" — that is, anyone who hits, teaches or talks the skill — decides to approach the art with "logic". Unfortunately, in the past I have found hitting discussion to be anything but logical. For example, a quick peek at Ted's career portrays him something like this: Named to Baseball's Hall of Fame in 1966; last of the .400 hitters with a .406 average in 1941; American League batting champion six times; home run champion four times; American League leader in total bases six times, in bases on balls eight times, in slugging percentage nine times; American League MVP in 1946 and 1949; and .304 hitter in 16 all-star games.

It is obvious from these statistics that Ted Williams was awesome. Now consider he had only average speed and lost five years in his prime due to military service; there is no doubt we are talking about possibly the greatest hitter who ever lived. Yet, despite Ted's credibility, it is interesting to note how quick the logic of today has labeled his approach to hitting as one that is unrealistic for the average young hitter. The tendency has been to call Ted a natural hitter, to cast him off as a talent phenomenon.

I hear this "natural hitter pitch" thrown at Williams all the time, and I think it's ridiculous. Ted Williams was *not* a talent phenomenon. Granted, the man did have good eyesight. Physically, however, many a hitter has come along who can be described as much faster and stronger with equal vision and a smaller strike zone. Certainly, he was not more fortunate than, say, Pete Rose or George Brett. Still, with their careers now over as well, you will find that they have not compiled the all-around stats of Williams. Why is that?

Ted Williams signed as a pitcher with San Diego standing 6'3" and weighing 148 pounds. What did Williams think when he looked in the mirror? It couldn't have mattered much because in the next three years he would become one of the best hitters in the American Association — hits, home runs, RBI's...everything. Remember: 6'3", 148 pounds! Where did his power come from?

In his younger years Ted grew up in San Diego, California which was, as he would say, "a place where a kid could stretch the baseball season to the depths of his imagination." While the California sun certainly played its role in his success, it's interesting to note that as a kid, Ted felt there were two boys in his neighborhood who were better than he was. Now, if you think about that for a minute, couldn't we assume that there was at least one kid in each of the other neighborhoods throughout California and across the rest of the country who had Williams' potential? Where does all this talent go?

I know one of the most important people in Williams' life was Rogers Hornsby (lifetime average .358, HR 302). Williams felt that Hornsby knew what it took to be a good hitter. So as a kid, looking up to Hornsby, Ted would constantly ask him questions, hoping to gather information that he could use to improve himself. One of the best hitting statements I've ever heard was one that Hornsby told Williams many years ago. Hornsby used to say, "Great hitters aren't born; they're made. They're made out of practice, fault-correction and confidence."

I feel that in Hornsby's words of wisdom my point starts to take shape. Quite possibly the greatest hitter in professional baseball history started his dream as a tall, slow, skinny kid with as many doubts and worries as any other. Despite his physical disadvantages, Ted Williams worked to realize his potential. When Ted reached the milestone of a successful baseball career, it just so happened that he was great. Maybe the greatest. If Ted Williams was truly a natural at something and it wasn't hitting a baseball, then it was drive...dedication. Ted Williams hit his potential through practice, fault-correction and confidence. But this process had begun long before he met Rogers Hornsby.

Fueled by a burning desire to be better than anyone, Ted Williams contributed something very important to the game. He pioneered and documented the first solid approach or technique for hitting a baseball. In the course of his journey to greatness he determined that potential was the sum of talent and technique. Faced with the fact that his talent could only be improved to a certain degree, he wisely chose to direct most his efforts toward his approach — toward technique, how to do it better!

What I'm saying is that Ted Williams, due to a lack of talent, was forced by his heart and ego to pursue the perfection of approach. This path, which rewarded Ted handsomely at various stages of his successful career, lured and eventually captured him. It locked him into a baseball life that to this day is filled with data, observation and research on the finer points of hitting. Ted's unique expedition to "discover hitting at its best" unquestionably crowns him as baseball's most accomplished and well-documented forefather of technical hitting. With his success relying mostly on approach, Ted Williams therefore becomes much more than a great hitter — he is a legitimate model of execution.

Where did all the other talented kids in all the other neighborhoods go? Why do hitters with more talent statistically lag behind? How does a tall, skinny kid hit for power and wind up being so successful at it? Questions like these can only be answered if you can comprehend

that the sport — the entire game of baseball — does not possess a clear picture of how successful hitting is pieced together. The game itself lacks a consistent approach or system to its "action-starting" skill.

Do you remember Danny Ainge? Why couldn't Danny Ainge hit in the major leagues? Any man who walked from the Toronto Blue Jays' infield onto the back court of the Boston Celtics had his share of ability. Why all the problems? Danny Ainge had trouble because he didn't execute properly. It's not that he couldn't have hit; it's that he didn't understand how to hit. Ainge could have been a fine hitter. The point here — there is more to hitting than just ability! Please, may this echo through each line to come. What brings one to reach potential is this — ability alongside proper execution. Due to the fact that Danny's obvious talents were stripped away when the task became putting a bat on a ball, I feel his career became an ideal case study reflecting the important relation between a player's ability and how it is perceived through the quality of their execution.

FIG 1-2. *Weak hitting Danny Ainge attemps to bunt during his tenure with the Toronto Blue Jays, before taking his place in the Boston Celtics basketball dynasty. Though Danny's genuine obvious talents were stripped away in the skill of hitting, his athletic career serves as an ideal case study reflecting the important relation between a player's real ability and how it is perceived through the quality of skill execution.*

The Globe and Mail, Toronto

What about Michael Jordan? Who in the world is more talented than Jordan? Name somebody, I'll get sandwiches... But the bottom line is this — when it came to hitting a baseball, he struggled.

Let's look at it a bit differently. I imagine that you could easily name for me twenty-five major league hitters right now who can't wear Jordan's sneakers in the talent department. But, would you bet me that Jordan could outhit any one of them? I'll bet not.

Baseball people who are quick to call Ted Williams a natural talent are merely searching for a source to explain his greatness. They are coming up with a way to justify something they don't understand. I bet they view David Copperfield as a natural too... While I can understand and sympathize with how and why this lack of hitting knowledge has come about, the fact remains that a good portion of baseball coaching is ironically retraining the finest hitting theory ever recorded.

As I take my shot at opening your eyes, please keep in mind one important factor — I didn't write this book because Ted was my hero or idol. I never saw him play. I never saw him on television. To me Ted Williams wasn't really a star, he was only a legend. He wasn't a Yaz, Rose, Kaline or Aaron; or for a kid today, make that a Griffy, Gwynn, Bonds or Walker. He was older — a man in black and white. This cowboy wasn't a Clint Eastwood, he was more a John Wayne. And to a young boy, the sunsets he rode into and the showdowns he had won were less impressive. Let's face it, to a kid seeing is believing. Ironically, this man merely represented another distant era of baseball, one that like all others played its role in creating the color and flare that has culminated in today's unsurpassed, double-knit millionaires.

AP/Wide World Photos

FIG 1-3. *Chicago Bulls superstar Michael Jordan meets a formidable opponent above when the task is putting a bat on a baseball. This basketball legend, the dominant force in the NBA year after year, was average at best as a minor league hitter.*

In 1980, as a sophomore at Bridgewater State College, my coach Fred Brown recommended me for a coaching position at the old Ted Williams Camp in the nearby town of Lakeville, Massachusetts. At the camp I worked with college and high school coaches from all over the country and taught hitting to players of various ages from all over the world.

At that point I had read "The Science of Hitting" about seventy times and two things were beginning to become evident: 1) I had not met anyone who understood Ted's theory as well as I did and 2) every level of play was missing out on a major enjoyment in the game of baseball — the thrill of hitting.

In 1980, hitting technique at the professional level was headed for a low. It was about that time I remember seeing Ted on television complaining about how "hitting had turned into horseshit." I knew exactly what he meant, but it seemed that no one else really understood.

At the Ted Williams Camp I noticed something much more important than professional baseball players throwing their potential away, I saw hundreds of enthusiastic ten-year-olds copying them... As a Physical Education major, I felt compelled to try and do something about it. The question was, what could I do?

That summer I met Ted Williams and he took a real liking to me. He told me that he wasn't sure if he had ever met anyone who knew as much about hitting as I did. I was twenty-one years old. I decided that fall that the best thing I could do for kids and for the game of baseball was to try and write a book about hitting from the viewpoint of not only a young hitter but a physical educator as well.

The next summer Ted read a rough draft of *Disciple of a Master: How to Hit a Baseball to Your Potential*. He met with me and said, "Christ, you've done a hell of a job with this. You've said some things in here much better than I had." He then asked me what he could do to help? I asked him to write the book's foreword and he agreed. Six years later I felt that *Disciple of a Master* was finally ready to be published. After drumming up the money to form a mini-publishing house — Line Drive Publishing — I put it into print in 1986.

Now, you may wonder why a twenty-one-year-old — especially one who had trouble spelling and drove a hundred dollar car — would try to defend and extend upon the theory of a living legend? Well, I could certainly tell you how Williams' theory stood up logically against the strict standards of the black board in my various Physical Education classes. Or I could tell you about results, how his theory helped not only me but hundreds of campers. Now looking back on it all, there are really only two reasons why I wrote that book. First, I could not stand the thought of others missing out on the pure fun of hitting a baseball correctly. And finally, in my initial meeting with Ted to discuss the book, he asked me why I was doing all of this. I sensed that he feared for me... like there was a possibility I wouldn't get very far with it. I told him that thousands of young players were being misled by poor technique on television. I told him that I was going to fight that battle. He said quickly, "Don't do it!" He said it as if it were an impossible task that had already made him weary. I then looked him dead in the eye and asked, "Have you had enough of all this?" He looked away and said, "You may not be too far off buddy."

That day it became obvious to me that Ted Williams had been beaten down by a changing trend — not just in hitting, but in baseball. Despite all he had done as a player and coach, baseball was moving in a direction that seemed to glorify his statistics but ignore his ideas. Baseball seemed to want his autograph but not his opinion. My teacher was discouraged, and that motivated me more than ever.

As you read this book it is very important that you understand the magic surrounding its origin. In the summer of 1980, at this boys camp just outside of Boston, the E.T. of hitting had for some unknown reason been mistakenly left on earth. At about the same time, the dreams of a young college player led him to the same location — baseball's arm of fate was about get a twist. Though light years apart, the two characters clearly became a team. The young player, somehow able to see beyond the aura of his amazing new friend, detected that he was troubled. Immediately, he searched for help only to find that there was no one more qualified than himself. Can you picture this? In short, Ted Williams needed to "phone home"... I was the kid with the bag of Reeses Pieces.

So where is hitting today? Well, it's on its way back! When I click on the television, catch a high school game or even a youth league game, I see things that make me think about hitting rather than the death of baseball. I'll never know how much of a role my book has played in this technical hitting comeback, but I've got a file of letters from a wide span of keen baseball minds assuring me that I've done my part. It was certainly six years well spent.

In *Hit Your Potential*, I'm going to show you why the Ted Williams' theory of hitting still remains the best approach for any type of hitter regardless of their size or ability. I'm also going to add in my ten years of hitting experience since the publication of *Disciple of a Master*.

And I've got to tell you, I'm excited about it. I'm excited because this time around I won't be trying to stop a technical hitting wave that's crashing against me; rather, I'll be adding to the height of a wave that all of baseball is ready to ride.

A PITCHING INCREASE OR A HITTING DECLINE?

At first I thought it would be easy. I figured by showing you a few graphs you too would immediately see the need for serious hitting renovation. Then I sadly realized that the majority of baseball accepts today's lack of hitting as the normal result of a pitching increase. This breaks down to mean that everything I'm about to say is for nothing if you believe that on average the hitters of today possess and execute a technique of hitting that is comparable or superior to that of the hitting in the past. Consider the question — Is it a pitching increase or a hitting decline?

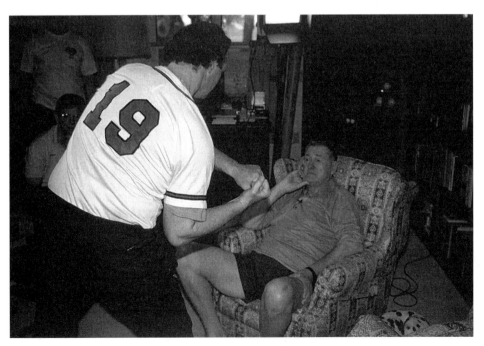

FIG 1-4. *Once again I take a lesson from the man himself as Ted Williams and I discuss hitting at his home in Hernando, Florida. Ted's passion for the subject is widely documented and here we find him giving me my third lesson of the day — the first two having come at the breakfast table.*

I'll agree that on the average pitchers throw the ball a bit faster; and must admit that man is getting bigger, stronger and quicker. Would anyone disagree with these claims? I also think the defense covers more ground for the same basic reasons. Certainly deepened fences have helped the pitcher, and relief pitching has been the man on the mound's best friend. The use of relief pitching is undoubtedly a more effective defense against hitting. In general, the skill of pitching has seen improvement due to an extended coaching emphasis focused specifically on this key aspect of the game.

But are these changes enough to place pitching head and shoulders above hitting? I say no. Hasn't hitting had its share of advantages to combat these factors? What about the lowering of the mound, the livening of the ball, Astroturf and the DH? Hasn't the hitter gotten stronger and quicker too, therefore allowing him to catch up to that faster pitch, reach those deepened fences and get down the line? Physically speaking, I don't believe that it has become any harder for a hitter to hit a pitcher. And I don't believe pitchers have gotten better.

Now, I'm not saying that pitching hasn't dominated the game statistically; we both know that it has. What I'm saying is that it should not have, because pitchers and hitters are men, and man's basic physical abilities increase as a race. Pitchers don't have a physical advantage. Their edge has formulated from the decrease of their rival skill. Pitching looks better because hitting has gotten worse.

The next question is obvious, "How did all this come about?" I'll explain that, but first let me say this. Many times when I hear people talking about baseball a lot of their talk is based on statistics. Such and such hit .327 with thirty-five home runs, this guy stole 32 bases, that guy

struck out 21 batters! It's fun and it's this kind of baseball language that gives us a quick picture of what happened. When we discuss approach, however, statistics are not as helpful. That's because a conversation regarding approach requires not only what happened, but also how it happened. I feel this is very important for you to understand.

Let me provide an example of what I mean. Assume that you and I play a game of one-on-one basketball. I, by my own choice, use nothing but jump shots and win 10-5. Then we play another game of basketball. This time, again by my own choice, I use nothing but hook shots and lose 10-5. After the games I go home and my friend calls me and says, "Hey, I watched those games of basketball that you played today and in the first game (using your jump shot) you shot 50 percent. "You were 10 for 20 and you won that game." He continues to explain, "In game two your hook shot was only hitting at 25 percent. You were 5 for 20. You lost that game." Shortly thereafter my friend makes a suggestion, "You should stop shooting the hook shot."

The next day you and I play again upon the suggestion of my friend. I decide to shoot only the jump shot and I win both games 10-5. I also continue to shoot at 50 percent.

If we look at my friend's win/loss statistics, they will show that after one day we are equal at 1-1. By day two we are not equal statistically as I am better at 3-1 to your 1-3. What made the difference between day one and day two? Was it my friend's input? Well, if your answer is yes, I agree. My friend convinced me with statistics to favor a better approach or technique. But notice how approach is not reflected anywhere in the statistics. It does not say that I won with my jump shot and lost with my hook shot.

If my friend did not phone me in this example, the win/loss statistics could have very well stayed equal. The truth is that on my own I may not have been able to decide on the better approach.

Let's go one step further. On day one I shot a total of 40 shots and 15 went in. On day two, I shot 40 shots and 20 went in. I was 25 percent better on day two but only because of my approach. Now is this approach factor reflected in the shooting statistics? No. In this example my friend has acted as what I refer to as a technical statistician. He has combined approach and result. He has combined the what happened and the how it happened.

Was your defense really equal to my offense on day one? No. My offense in game two was played with a sub-par approach. But in a record book, day one can only be seen and remembered as equal — record books do not display approach.

When I say that hitting has gotten worse, what I mean is that on average it is not approached as efficiently as it used to be in comparison to its defense. Much like my hook shot, hitting chose a weaker approach or technique for a good thirty years. Unfortunately, there were no technical statisticians to help direct the approach of hitting back onto course. Baseball had recorded the what happened and not the how it happened. Consequently, the skill of hitting a baseball suffered and has setbacks in execution to blame.

How did this all come about? After great deliberation, I place the blame for the decline of hitting on the changes within the skill's learning environment. In my experience as both a student and teacher, I have found any successful learning environment to contain the following educational components: 1) enthusiasm on the learner's behalf to learn; 2) reliable information, along with someone qualified to transmit it; 3) "experimentation time," that is, a special time of practice and/or study where the learner tries to understand the worth of what he's been taught; and 4) a setting clear of unnecessary pressure and distraction. Due to the quality of its educational components, my claim is that the learning environments of yesterday, on average, were far superior and therefore responsible for the success of the hitters who grew from them. While it is impossible to pick one year that marks the beginning of this gradual learning change, if we compare the average learning environment of 1940 to today, I'm sure you'll see the iron in my words.

FIG 1-5. *Enthusiam is a key ingredient of success in any learning environment. Dan O'Reilly brought plenty of it to the practice fields and game diamonds of the newly formed Ted Williams League.*

FIG 1-6 & 1-7. *All of my camps and clinics are designed with the characteristics of a good learning environment in mind. The hitting clinic shown above was held on the grounds of the Ted Williams Museum and Hitters Hall of Fame in Hernando, Florida.*

In 1940, baseball as a form of entertainment and boyish recreation was unmatched. Baseball was truly the national pastime, and therefore the enthusiasm to become an accomplished hitter was at its peak. Baseball was everywhere. Believe it or not at that time there were 43 minor leagues — more than 244 cities and towns supported teams! Kids and adults took more pride in playing and understanding the game because baseball was truly the nation's #1 interest. Kids taped up old balls and nailed broken bats back together while fans sincerely lived and died with baseball's teams and players.

Today the enthusiasm to learn is watered down. Baseball has competition ranging from multiple levels of sports on numerous cable stations to the World Wide Web. Baseball is no longer the national pastime. Today there are very few minor leagues. Largely due to the invention of television, the number of minor league baseball players decreased 70 percent from 1948 to 1963.

Kids and adults simply do not take as much of an interest in baseball as they used to. On the contrary, most youngsters develop an interest in a variety of pastimes — television, video games, the latest trends. It's become a rarity to find kids taping up old balls or bats in order to play a backyard game. Fans don't live and die with baseball's teams and players like they used to. People's interests and energies are simply distributed by choice over a wider array of choices.

Reliable hitting information was easier to come by back in 1940. To begin with, you had great professional role models — true ballplayers. A kid going to see a major league game back then was getting his money's worth. Magazines, newspapers, and radio sources featured the high-quality tips that these players passed on. (This as opposed to broadcasting the wild antics and indisgretions we see today.) The result — such pointers were utilized effectively by inspired young hitters, coaches and parents.

You must understand that in 1940 the experience level of the general public was much higher — more people had tried to hit a baseball. In those times baseball had a popularity similar to the Hula-hoop or Frisbee during the late sixties. Everyone had tried it to some degree and many had opinions about just how to do it. It was more an activity of the time.

Certainly you'd agree that various activities have been more popular and better executed in their respective era. I mean, if you were picking the all-time kids team to play marbles, for instance, you'd never pick a kid from the 90's That's because kids in the 90's simply don't play marbles. Now when it comes to your all-time skateboarding or snowboarding team... that's a different story.

Today we have very few professional role models; as a result, we do not have as much reliable information being passed on to the learner. But I think hitting is on its way back and I mean it. In the past few years I have witnessed a positive change at the professional level which I am proud to report. I have also seen improvements in the instructional hitting materials accessible in a variety of forms. This is progress. Please don't get the wrong idea, however; despite these recent improvements, by my standards the current state of hitting is all still below average.

Ironically, we are equipped more now than ever to communicate effectively. Just look around — videos, books, magazines, computer publications, the internet, CD ROM, hundreds of television stations. By merely manipulating the button on a remote control you can now absorb all sorts of hitting information, at both the professional and college level. Unfortunately, what you come across is likely to be behind the times.

Possibly the greatest learning plus of 1940 was the tendency to experiment and be creative. Think of it this way, in the days of radio you had to imagine what was happening in a game and then figure out why. I think that kind of questioning and answering approach can result in learning at its best. Also, the decade that follows a depression tends to spawn kids that know necessity as the mother of invention. These boys would create different sandlot games for any number of players or amounts of available equipment.

FIG 1-8. *This group of young men certainly had a sense of experimentation — the Norwell, Massachusetts plate study crew. Day in and day out they were asked to play the game of baseball under the unique set of rules outlined by the study. Was it a different game? No. But was it executed differently? Yes. These players handled the challenge exceptionally and helped to lay a foundation for the Ted Williams League of today. I will never forget this crew of kids and my assistant, Roger Snow.*

FIG 1-9. *Distractions and pressures are common in organized youth play. Here we find a player turning for a candid camp photo. The only problem is that he is in the batter's box awaiting the delivery of the next pitch. This sort of situation, which happens often in games and practice due to the interference of a parent or fan, is discouraged. Remember, the game belongs to the kids – let 'em play.*

Today you can forget about experimentation and creative learning because kids aren't as self-entertaining — they don't have to be. In our days, mothers and fathers pay networks, video games and servers handsomely to entertain the minds of their children. As a result, many kids have become watchers as opposed to doers, copiers rather than creators.

I'm also convinced that organized youth baseball (1946) has put its squash on experimentation. Youth baseball provides too much ill-guided instruction that takes away from the learner's natural instinct to sample different potential solutions. Certainly, structured youth play has retired a good portion of those sandlot games; and later I'll even show you how several of its poorly-calculated dimensions also limit the learning of this skill.

Distractions were at a minimum in 1940. You didn't have kids being pulled by that elaborate selection of pastimes. There just weren't the same pressures that there are today. Kids generally played with familiar friends, the neighborhood gang. Organized youth baseball brought the critical eye of adults and strangers into a kid's atmosphere of play. Hey, it's one thing when your pal next door says you stink, but it's another thing altogether when it's his father or the kid across town.

The controversy over correct technique is an enormous pressure today. Everybody and their uncle thinks they know just how it's done; as a result, the learner doesn't know who or what to trust. The market is flooded with so-called coaching aids and learning tools designed and sold by countless people who, by all rights, should be wearing clownsuits in this circus-like atmosphere.

My conclusion is that the positive learning environments of yesterday regressed as a result of the changes within society. Society was growing towards variety, not only in sport, but also in recreation and entertainment. With this dramatic cut in baseball interest (not necessarily in numbers, mind you, but surely in depth), it wasn't long before the learning components I spoke of began to distort or deteriorate. It's really all very understandable. When you combine a loss of interest with the learning needs of the hardest single act in sports, it isn't long before you have a lack of knowledge and execution. It is a hitting decline.

A CHANGE AT THE TOP

Where is hitting today? After the cut of the minor league system starting in 1949, professional baseball became thoroughbred baseball. With teams signing fewer players — again a cut reaching up to 70 percent — the tendency became to sign only those who possessed exceptional ability. The criteria for professional consideration resorted to a reliance on God-given talents, like foot speed, quickness and strength. Out of line with Roger Hornsby's belief, pro baseball began to invest in hitters who "were born" and not those who "were made". The money once spent to harvest good execution was now used to find and sign raw talent. Superior ability replaced and eliminated a good portion of the teaching phase.

Unfortunately, when these exceptional athletes came up to the big time, their abilities could not keep up with the hitting pace set by the superior execution of the past. Though, on the average, they were physically above the hitters before them, their lack of approach against the stability and growth of pitching put them on a level inferior. Obviously, this lack of approach was more than apparent to the older hitters. These players, many times finishing their careers in the minors or opting to coach, did put forth a concerned effort to help, but the thoroughbreds wouldn't listen. Being the cream of the crop and potentially superior to the older hitters, their apprehension and ego created a stick-to-your-guns attitude. They decided to hang with the techniques that had brought them into professional baseball. Unfortunately and unknowingly, they turned their backs on good advice.

Now, this wasn't always the case; some young players did recognize their lack of technical quality and wanted to learn. However, the cutback of the minor leagues had taken away their experimentation time and added a hundred pounds of pressure. (When a major league team has only four farm teams below it as opposed to 20, the name of the game is "up or out.") The days of learning and seasoning in pro baseball had gone. The focus had become immediate production rather than catered potential — a trade of overall talent for the quality of technique. In time, the hitters with the better techniques retired, and major league baseball slowly but surely became plagued with exceptional athletes possessing makeshift approaches. Who pays the price?

Well, not only does the professional never reach his potential, but as a result the hitters on all the levels below don't either. Let's not forget; pro baseball is at the top of the baseball totem pole! It is copied and respected as the finest example of execution by all the leagues below it. With this decline of technique, suddenly major league players everywhere began passing on bits and pieces of conflicting advice. For example, one player may believe in the downswing, while another found success with a level swing. The result is a teaching and learning fiasco where the awe of pro baseball towers over logic.

Before long we ended up with thousands of players and coaches with only average ability copying the subordinate approaches of major league players with exceptional ability. Ironically, these approaches not only restrained the professional hitter himself, but also slaughtered flocks of starry-eyed followers. Regardless of the sport, athletes who possess extraordinary talent are the least likely to refine approach because they have survived a good portion of their lives on talent alone.

Am I trying to down major league baseball? Absolutely not. Major league baseball showcases some of the most talented players in the world and does so in baseball's most exciting forum. Thousands and thousands of people from every walk of life look to major league baseball to provide a clean form of American entertainment and year after year major league baseball comes through.

But is it the business of professional baseball to provide the very best of baseball execution? Not necessarily. The objective of business oriented baseball is to provide baseball that makes money. The person professional baseball is designed for is the fan. The average fan is not trying to be a hitter or a fielder. He's trying to relax. He's got a job and maybe a family. He's not a kid but, on average, much older — old enough to drink beer and buy razor blades, old enough to stay up late to watch the end of the game. Somewhere in pro baseball's business records it has been determined that the average fan does not really understand and therefore does not appreciate refined technique. And they are absolutely right.

A closer look shows us that the front office must also provide an entertaining on-the-field product — within the scope of its financial boundaries. It is money in versus money out.

Whether a team wins a world championship or not, the money a team generates due to ticket sales is limited. On the other hand, player salaries seem to become less and less limited. Many teams simply can't afford to pay for great hitting. Certainly pro baseball has to keep an eye on the production of its players and the market value of such production. In relation to its current financial status and future projections, teams can only afford to employ a certain degree of hitting prowess.

Obviously there is nothing wrong with this line of thought in the world of business. If you and I were running a house painting company, wouldn't we paint the houses in a manner that made the owner (the fan) happy and us (the front office) a profit? Sure we would. We'd be business fools to embrace concepts that have been determined to be of no benefit to our objective. We must also keep in mind our financial limits. For instance, we could not hire or train dozens of top-notch painters (hitters) if we could only realistically afford two. You'll find that the automobile industry thinks like this. Fast food businesses do, too. Why would the case be any different in baseball?

With hitting on its way back I am curious to see what will happen. I mean, if hitting production starts to really climb, which it may, who is going to pay for it? You can't increase the ticket prices because in theory the fan won't pay for something he or she doesn't understand or appreciate. I don't think it will come out of the players. The team owners are not going to give away profits. Unfortunately, I think we will be forced to see an alteration in the game itself — a deadening of the ball or a heightening of the mound — something that will dull hitting production and counter the cost of a better approach.

The problem here lies in the assumption that professional players have reached their potential and that professional baseball is obligated to bring them to that point. This is simply not true. Therefore, it should never again be assumed that the business of baseball is modeling a high level of execution for the sport of baseball. When you consider their objectives it really does not make sense for them to have this responsibility. Likewise, it does not make sense for the sport of baseball to look to the business of baseball for this response.

Why run amuck about all this crap? Why not just talk about hitting? Well, I'd love to, but unfortunately it would not be enough to do the trick! Baseball needs an overall understanding of the big picture. It needs to know what has gone on in the past and what is going on today to prevent the possibility of another hitting setback.

Have you ever heard the "Charlie Lau theory of hitting"? Charlie Lau, formerly a batting instructor for the Kansas City Royals, wrote a book in the early eighties entitled, *The Art of Hitting .300.* Not only was a good portion of its contents illogical, but (and more aggravating) it was popular for all the wrong reasons.

In 1980 Royals' star George Brett neared the .400 mark with a .390 batting average. At the time he was one of pro baseball's premier hitters and all-around players. While I'm sure Lau was of some assistance to Brett's success, George Brett did not use the theory that the Lau book described in the major leagues. He did, however, demonstrate Lau's approach in the pictures of Lau's book and therefore associated his success with those movements.

In summary, at a point in baseball history where hitting was already struggling due to society's effect on its learning environment, we now had a big-league batting instructor teamed with pro baseball's most popular hitter harvesting a hitting approach that had been grown in weakened soil. It was eagerly accepted and devoured by the game of baseball.

As far as I am concerned that book led hitting a baseball from the frying pan to the fire. It was only accepted as a reliable learning source due to the popularity and fanfare of a baseball business that does not specialize in approach. Where is the Lau theory today? It is out of professional baseball. Discarded! Determined by its own players to be of no value. (It is unfortunate but at the amateur levels, where change takes more time, this theory is still very much alive; therefore, I will continue to attack it as its weaknesses become relative.)

FIG 1-10. *When we shot the video, "Hitting the Ted Williams Way" (Part One), there was a segment which called for my participation as a hitter. I was truly touched when the crowd offered a warm round of applause after I had taken my swings.*

My underlying point — what is to stop this from happening again? Could another business-blinded tag team stand on the shoulders of major league marketing and block the progress of this great game? It could happen tomorrow!

What about pro players who run instructional camps and clinics? Players and coaches are two different things. Are they skill builders? Some are. Most, however, are not. You wouldn't hire a race car driver to rebuild your engine would you? No. You would hire a mechanic and hopefully a damn good one! Are you paying for instruction or, realistically, for a form of memorabilia?

I pick at the pro players, but college coaches may very well be even more guilty here. For one thing there are more of them. Head coach-ing at the college level is a big responsibility, not to mention the commitment toward the academic lives of their players. On the average, I have found these people to be recruiters and organizers — not skill builders. But, they do have the use of the college facility, the field looks great, and ten of their players are helping out in uniform. The kids are in the dorm and its all you can eat... I'd go.

Only awareness can protect your approach. Who is showing you? What are they showing you? And why? Here I've tried to provide you with a solid learning environment. I will try to eliminate your distractions and equip you with reliable information for all the right reasons. Welcome back to the popularity of logic and the fanfare of common sense.

FIG 1-11. *In 1987 I published* **Disciple of a Master,** *my original attempt at documenting a successful approach to hitting based on the Ted Williams model. Here I am pictured posing for a local news photographer around the time that book came out. Later that year I went out to dinner with Ted and, in addition to our discussion of hitting, he rifled me about the beard you see here... "Clean it up a little!" he said. Let's just say that I haven't grown it back since.*

The Mental Work Of Successful Hitting

KNOW HOW IT ALL FITS

In teaching the skill of hitting, I have found that the best results come from detailed explanations coupled with the individual hitter's natural progression. That is to say, it's best for the student to clearly understand what he's doing and why he's doing it before he moves on to something new. While it's true that you can work faster by simply fixing a hitter's weakness or weaknesses, I don't view that sort of repair work as quality instruction. Although the hitter may be an all-star while you're helping him, he's sure to fade when you leave. Then, without guidance, he will lack the knowledge to get back on the right track.

Now, you may think I'm making this sound more dramatic than it really is; honestly, I'm not. When potential is the goal, knowledge is a must. I'm talking about having the ability to make the right corrections and adjustments — the ability to self-coach. Hey, if you're playing a double-header in the middle of August, the sun beating down at 85 degrees, and the first time up you feel late on every pitch, you'd best be able to figure out why. A double-header could cost you ten poor at-bats — ten poor at-bats! A hitter who can make the proper adjustments may only end up with one poor at-bat. Maybe he can adjust during that first time up and then finish the day with ten quality at-bats. The hitter who can't make the proper corrections and adjustments is far below his personal par. This hitter will spend too much time pondering over the answers to elementary questions, not to mention those valuable at-bats he'll waste modeling flashpan advice. Knowing right from wrong and the reasons behind both is the place to be. This is why a good batting instructor is invaluable. If a guy knows his stuff, he can detect and correct problems before they plague the hitter. By playing guardian angel to the entire lineup, a good batting instructor can eliminate pounds of pressure and instill tons of confidence.

FIG 2-1. *Former major leaguer Mike Epstein, who played for the Washington Senators and was coached by Ted Williams, speaks to a group of kids at a Steve Ferroli summer program. This was a great opportunity for the players to hear some of the same ideas from a different source. Eventually, all of these players will be on their own without an instructor standing there to fix problems for them. These players will have to know how it all fits!*

Unfortunately, good batting instructors are a rarity. Therefore the knowledge of the developing skill must come from the hitter. With this in mind, I have written this book much like I teach — in progressive detail. When it comes to hitting a baseball, I want you to know how to do it properly and I want you to know why certain approaches work and others do not. I want you to learn how to coach yourself and eventually develop the confidence to teach others.

A FEW DEFINITIONS

One of the hitting world's greatest problems is the inaccurate definitions of hitting terminology. Add to this the fact that the hitting world tends to underdefine, and the confusion is amplified. I feel it's important for you to see how I define certain hitting terms to avoid any misunderstanding. This should make it much easier for the hitter and coach to understand and then apply what is discussed in this book.

Hitting: Hitting is the seasonal battle of mind and body against the opposing team's pitchers and defense in a game situation.

Technique-Approach: A good hitting technique or approach is a logical batting philosophy combined with sensible and effective mechanics used by the hitter in such a way that will not only allow him to hit the ball as hard and as often as possible, but will also allow the hitter to reach the maximum of total bases by hit, walk or error.

Talents: Talents in hitting are the tools that make up the hitter's capabilities. A hitter's talents are both mental and physical and together both dictate his potential. These include attitude, intelligence, observational powers, patience, vision, coordination, quickness, foot speed, strength, stature and endurance.

ATTITUDE IS NO. 1

When I think of the perfect hitting attitude, I think of a movie. In a scene from "Rocky II", Rocky's trainer, Mickey, is telling Rocky (a left-handed fighter) that he must learn to fight right-handed to protect a bad eye and confuse his opponent. When his trainer finishes, Rocky says, "Hey, Mick, I can't learn to fight right-handed no more," and Mickey says, "What's can't? There ain't no can't."

As a batter, unless you're just beginning to hit for the first time, chances are you will have to make some changes or adjustments. They may be mental or they may be mechanical, but they won't be easy. You may want to say, "I can't." Don't do it! If you want to be a hitter, remember "there ain't no can't"!

What is "can't"? Quite simply, it is a cop-out word that implies laziness or fear of failure. It is an easy way out and a convenient quitter's phrase. It is also a word that has no room in a hitter's vocabulary. "Can" is a much better substitute, implying self-confidence and determination. When we speak of the "can" and "can't" viewpoints of anything, we are basically speaking about the most common ingredient in any success recipe — *attitude*.

Except for health or eyesight, the most prevailing ingredient necessary for successful hitting is a positive attitude. If you're going to have any shot at all at becoming a good hitter, you must maintain a progressive and inquisitive attitude. You have to want to get better and hunger to know how to make it happen. Remember, we're talking about becoming superior at a very complex skill. You have to love it. While coaching the Washington Senators, Ted was known for inspiring desire, provoking conversation and stimulating thought on the topic of hitting. As a player, they used to say that Williams lived for his next time at bat. He wanted to hit, he wanted to be great, and he wished it on every falling star. Good hitters must want to be good hitters, because the odds are stacked strongly against a hitter's progression and success. I hope I'm coming in loud and clear when I say, "If you don't want it, you won't get it."

In hitting, more than in other skills, the desire and dedication has to be amplified in the player. That's because unlike other sports, a hitter isn't going to get the proper instruction, practice or support he needs to improve. Therefore it is an absolute must for the hitter to nurture a positive attitude that reflects a dedicated and determined psychological foundation. The hitter must be like a shark — his survival thriving on both his insatiable curiosity and relentless motivation toward progress. It is this attitude and this attitude alone that will enable a hitter to battle the modern challenge of learning proper technique and then utilizing it to reach hitting potential.

Think about it. If you want to become proficient at a difficult task, you best have a crackerjack attitude to tackle it. You wouldn't fish for tuna with five-pound test line, nor would

FIG 2-2. *The hitter must be like a shark – his survival thriving on both insatiable curiousity and relentless motivation.*

you hunt elephant with a BB gun. Likewise, it's important that you don't try to become a hitter with a pin-the-tail-on-the-donkey approach.

GET A GOOD PITCH

After sewing the seeds for a good hitting attitude, your next goal is to understand the mental work behind a hitter's success. In *The Science of Hitting*, Ted said that hitting a baseball was 50 percent from the neck up. He claimed first and foremost that a smart hitter must get "a good pitch to hit. " But is it a high pitch? A low pitch? Inside? Outside? Or right down the pipe? Is it a curve ball? A fastball? A slider? What is a good pitch to hit?

Off the top of my head, I'd define a good pitch as one you have not only anticipated but one that also happens to come within an area of the strike zone which is appealing in relation to the count. While this definition conveys the basic idea, I'm afraid that unless we break it down, most will never really come to grips with the value of the statement.

ANTICIPATION

Let's take a look at the word *anticipate*. To anticipate in hitting is to guess or to look for a particular pitch before it has been thrown. Make no mistakes here, with less than two strikes I'm talking about an all-out decision to prepare for one type of pitch and only that pitch. If another one comes, I'm not going to swing. I will take that pitch even if it's a strike. I know, I hear it all the time. You're wondering, "Why guess? Why not just hit whatever is thrown?" You figure if the pitcher has three pitches, two-thirds of the time you'll be off; and at that rate, taking strikes left and right.

FIG 2-3. *When a hitter gets to the park, he has but one thing on his mind – the pitcher. Here a former player of mine, Jaime Quiros, winds up for the showdown in a Boston Park League all-star game at Fenway Park.*

A hitter guesses for the sake of timing, and I'll soon talk about timing in more detail. For now, please make a mental note that hitters also guess because it gives them a much greater chance of hitting the different pitches they must face. The hitter facing a pitch that he has not anticipated is at a grave disadvantage. The speed of the unexpected pitch will jog the hitter's timing. If the count is 2-and-0 and you guess fastball and a fat curve comes right down the pipe, a good hitter will take that pitch because it is not what he is looking for and therefore not what he is prepared to hit. The hitter's body is in no position to hit that pitch with authority. With less than two strikes, a good pitch to hit must be a pitch you have anticipated.

If the pitcher has the ability to throw different speed pitches, doesn't it seem logical that the hitter should try to prepare or adjust for the probable speed? You bet it does. In simple terms, that's what timing is. Unfortunately, the hitter doesn't know what's coming; and therefore, in order for the hitter to prepare himself mechanically, he must first consciously decide what pitch is probable... He must guess.

As far as accurate guessing goes, I would like you to think about another Ted Williams statement. Ted said, *"The beautiful thing about baseball is that the hardest pitches to hit are the hardest pitches to throw."* To me, that remark is brilliant because it isolates the true battle between the pitcher and hitter and alleviates some of the doubt over a hitter's ability to think along with the pitcher. Hey, when the count is 2-and-0, the pitch most likely will be a fastball; and when the count is 0-and-2, the pitch will probably be a breaking ball. And why? Because fastballs are easier to throw and breaking balls are harder to hit. There's no big secret, it's simple logic. For the most part, when the pitcher is behind in the count, like 2-and-0, he isn't going to risk throwing a pitch that is more difficult to control. Why risk letting the count go to 3-and-0 and then be pressured to throw the strike? More times than not the pitcher will come to you. Remember, *"a walk is as good as a hit,"* and because of this you can count on certain pitches at certain times. A .300 hitter fails seven out of ten times — seven out of ten times! Unless the hitter is a true long-ball threat in a tight situation, the pitcher would be foolish not to throw the fastball 2-and-0. As you will hopefully begin to realize, guessing along with the pitcher is not a difficult task.

Naturally, as you advance in baseball, pitchers tend to throw pitches that are not probable. Sometimes the pitcher will be throwing his breaking ball just as consistently as his fastball, maybe even more so. Please don't misunderstand me. I'm not saying when you have a 2-and-0 count you always look for the fastball; or when it's 0-and-1, you must look for the offspeeds. I just want you to understand where the bulk of your anticipation should be based.

Years ago Ted said that guessing came from a framework — a framework created by observing the pitcher and storing up information for future use. It's not really guessing at all. The term "guessing" implies a decision based on luck or chance. I'm talking about a calculation — a calculation based on the review of data. Ted referred to this as doing your homework. He felt the hitter's past and present observations would enable him to think properly at the plate — enable him to guess correctly. Let's face it, all pitchers are different, and if you're going to get to know their tendencies, you've got to take notice — you've got to watch. I know that's a hard thing for many guys, but that's the way it is. They're not going to throw the good one all the time; and therefore, observation is a key. It gives us our game plan for each at-bat.

As far as I'm concerned there are three main observational times of equal importance: 1) when the pitcher is warming up, 2) when you're at the plate and 3) when the pitcher is pitching to someone else. During these times the hitter will begin to do his homework. The hitter will ask and answer certain questions about the pitcher. For example: What is his style? I mean is he a cutey, a challenger or is he a little of both? Is his wind-up deceptive? What about his stretch? How many pitches is he warming up? How many is he using? How many are strikes? Is a certain pitch generally up or down? What is his best pitch? What does he think his best pitch is? What pitch does he use at specific counts? Does he pitch differently with runners in stealing position? How did he pitch you last time and what happened? Is there something on his mind like a home run, passed ball or wild pitch? What pitch was it on? Is he constantly concerned with details such as the positioning of a certain fielder, the condition of the mound or a short fence? Is the weather or wind in his favor or yours? What is his attitude? Has something changed it?

I talk about the pitcher but it may be more accurate to focus these question on the battery — that is to say the pitcher and the catcher. After all, the catcher is generally the player who is calling the pitches. I think the pitcher (at all levels) has lost a great deal of his shaking off clout over the years. I think it is an unforeseen side effect that has surfaced from the designated hitter rule. The mentality here — the pitcher does not know as much about the mentality of the hitter because he no longer hits for himself in the American League. Most times the pitch selection is solely the decision of the catcher. So these questions and others should really be directed toward the battery.

The answers to these and similar questions will help you to narrow down the odds as to what pitch is coming and why. You'll be thinking along with the battery for the game and for the season. For example, let's say you watch the pitcher warm up and he only shows two pitches, a fastball and a curve (this is often the case in high school baseball). He faces two hitters before you and throws three curves in the dirt. You step up to the plate and the first pitch is a fastball outside; you say to yourself, "Well, the curve hasn't been over, so I'm guessing fastball." The pitcher throws it and you hit a home run. Now, the next time up you say to yourself, "No way will he throw me the fastball." You're assuming that because you tagged him for a homer, he'll bring the curve and so you guess first pitch curve. This time he throws the curve for a strike. Now you say, "Well, he's up in the count by throwing the curve and since I hit the fastball last time, I'm going to guess curve again." Here it comes, bang, line out to the shortstop; but you're proud of a good at-bat due to logical thinking.

On the other hand, what if he had struck you out in that first at-bat with a called fastball and two swinging curves. Well, in your second at-bat you would be likely to see a first-pitch curve as well. Remember not only are you looking at them but they are looking at you. They are waiting for you to show them how to get you out. If he missed with the curve, then he would most likely go back to the fastball. That is to say that the 1-and-0 count would scare him back to the comfort of the fastball. If it was a strike, he would try the curve again at 1-and-1 and so on.

Obviously, these are basic examples, and the tendency is for many people to claim that, "Yeah, when there are only two pitches, guessing can be easy. But when you get to the col-

lege or pro level where you find three and four pitches, you can't guess." I think these people are selling themselves or their players short. When you learn and feel the benefits of a good swing, observation, and guessing (again, something that's been lost today), you won't be so quick to throw all this credit toward the pitcher. His ability and pitch selection won't be so impressive because your decisions and movements will make you quicker, stronger and more consistent.

FIG 2-4. *From the time a hitter enters the ballpark, his sights are set on ballpark enemy number one, the pitcher. Here we see the viewpoint of a hitter facing former Red Sox pitching great, Roger Clemens.*

Also, when you're a good hitter, it gets much harder for the pitcher to mix his pitches up — that is, to risk throwing something other than his best. Sure, he might have four pitches, but when you're a good hitter he starts to worry about throwing his lower-quality pitches. When a hitter establishes himself with the pitching in his league it makes it easier to guess because the pitching tends to challenge him with their very best rather than an arsenal of different pitches.

LOCATION

What is an acceptable location in relation to the count? It is no more than playing the percentages; that is, striving for a ball that is deserving of our swing with regard to the situation. I feel getting good location is best executed by setting up three hitting areas. The first area is called the *rip area*. It is the area in which the hitter feels he can hit his best, and it should encompass about a third of the hitter's strike zone. The rip area will be used when the hitter is up on the count. The hitter will now refrain from swinging even at an anticipated pitch that is not in his rip area, and that's important. Figure 2-5a shows my personal rip area. However, keep in mind that yours may be totally different, as seen with a different hitter in Figure 2-6a.

The second area will merely be an extension of the rip area and will not only include the rip area but will include two-thirds of your strike zone. This second area, which I call the *even area*, will be used on all counts with one strike or when the hitter feels the count is even. Figure 2-5b outlines both my rip and even areas, while Figure 2-6b outlines the other hitter. Again, the hitter would not swing at an anticipated pitch that was outside the even area.

The third area is your strike zone and also includes what Ted calls the gray area; that being the area around the strike zone where strikes are sometimes called balls and balls are sometimes called strikes. This area is used whenever the hitter has two strikes on him. Figures 2-5c and 2-6c outline all three of the areas, including the gray area.

I think you can understand the importance of using these areas correctly. According to Ted, *"a good hitter can hit a pitch in a good spot three times better than a great hitter can hit a ball in a questionable spot."* If I go up to the plate and ground out on a 2-and-0 pitch on the outside corner at my knees (a place where I don't hit as well as others), I'm a fool! I have literally helped the pitcher to get me out. Ted will say that pitchers are lucky to face hitters so dumb, and he's right.

Nothing is easy and, unfortunately, there is still one more very important factor. Ted called it knowing yourself. In Ted's book there is a great hitting statement by Lefty O'Doul. O'Doul, another great hitter, said that most hitting faults come from a lack of knowledge, uncertainty and fear; and that boils down to knowing yourself. Knowing yourself means knowing your strengths and weaknesses. Do you hit the curve ball well? Is the high fastball a problem? Do you have trouble picking up the slider? Truthfully knowing the answers to these questions and questions like them will dictate whether you know yourself or not, and this becomes important when defining a good pitch to hit. The reason I say this is because your definition of a good pitch to hit can change daily when you compare the pitcher's strengths and weaknesses to your own. For example, if the curve ball is your major weakness and you're facing a good curve ball pitcher, you'll probably be better off waiting for the fastball. A step further, you may look for that fastball in the even area when you're up on the count. You may decide to concede some location on the fastball to avoid your weakness with the curve.

On the other hand, if you're facing a pitcher whom you can completely handle, then you're going to wait for the anticipated pitch in the areas we described.

Each time you play, your definition of a good pitch to hit will be based on the pitcher's strengths and weaknesses in relation to yours and, like a poker hand, each pitcher will have to be played a bit differently.

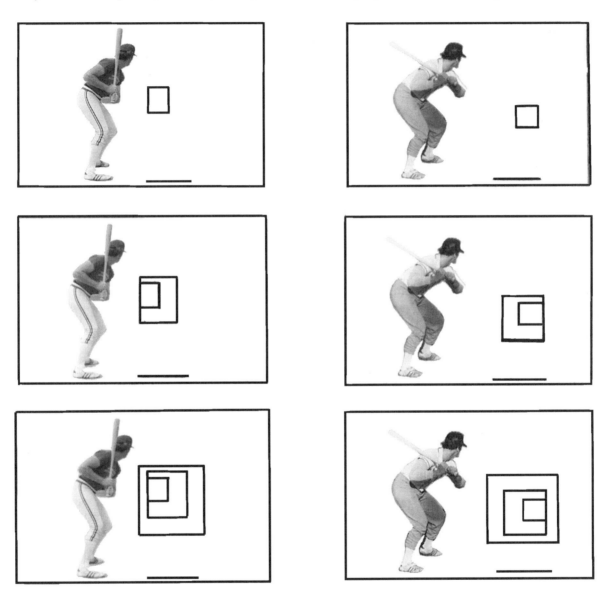

FIG 2-5 (a-c, top to bottom). *2-5a shows the rip area, the zone the hitter hits best and the area in which a hitter should focus when ahead in the count. 2-5b includes the even area, an extension of the rip area, and the zone to focus on with a one-strike count. 2-5c displays the relationship between both these areas inside the strike zone.*

FIG 2-6 (a-c, top to bottom). *2-6a shows the rip area for a different style of hitter whose mechanics lead him to prefer an alternate area when ahead in the count. 2-6b includes this hitter's rip area and even area. 2-6c displays the relationship between both these areas for a hitter who has adopted this particular style.*

HOW TO SEE

After understanding the requirements of a "good pitch to hit," we must learn the finer points of reading the pitch to decipher both what it is and where it is. We must learn how to see. After the pitch is released, the hitter will begin to absorb information in a split second. Fortunately, when this information is processed correctly, it will enable the hitter to identify the type of pitch and its location. Because most pitches travel at different speeds, speed is the first clue when trying to identify the type of pitch. To identify a pitch by its speed, the hitter must grow accustomed to determining the oncoming pitch's speed in relation to the speed of the pitch he had anticipated. The feeling he'll receive will answer the question, "Are you on time?" which is much like asking "Have you guessed correctly?" or "Are you getting what you anticipated?" I call this reading or answering period *timing feel*. Because a solid understanding of timing feel requires more mechanical discussion, let's put it on hold until we discuss the term timing in more detail. However, please keep in mind that a pitch's speed is the first clue in its identification.

The next clue is the look of the ball — the spin and color. After the speed checks out, the rotation and color can make all the difference in the world. Take the curve and straight change, for example. Because they may be traveling at the same speed, the hitter watching a straight change, waiting for it to break, may end up being late. However, if the hitter was able to identify this pitch as a straight change by its color and rotation, it's likely the hitter wouldn't have waited as long. Certainly the slider has a unique spin as opposed to the fastball — a crucial clue in its identification.

There is one other type of clue that a hitter may also receive — a tip-off. Ted spoke of how he could sometimes immediately identify a curve by the way certain pitchers really had to snap it off to get it going. These motion clues, or tip-offs, are impurities in the pitcher's delivery that give a pitch away, and naturally they can be a great advantage. However, I don't believe they happen often enough to make them a major concern. For our purposes, I'll say that if a pitcher gives something away, fine; however, don't spend time looking for or trying to invent a tip-off that is not there. As we've discussed, there are better things to be concerned with.

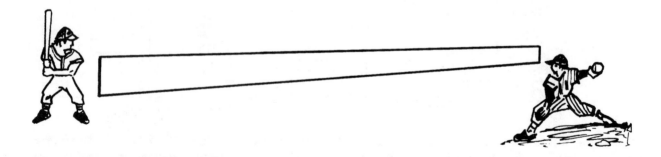

FIG 2-7. *The hitter should think of the ball as though it were traveling in a tunnel. This will allow the hitter to recognize the relationship between the earlier points along the ball's flightpath and the strike zone.*

To determine location, I feel that it is good practice for every hitter to think about the ball as if it's traveling in a tunnel. This tunnel starts out small over the pitcher's shoulder and increases almost to the size of the hitter's strike zone. Figures 2-7 and 2-8 show what I mean from two different angles. To master the use of good location a hitter must begin to learn where a pitch will end up (in his or out of his strike zone) by noticing a relation between the ball's location when it's passing through an early point in the tunnel, and then its location at the plate. I call this *tunneling*. The advantage of this lies in the fact that a tunneling hitter can see a pitch at one point in time and understand where it will be at another. The hitter is able to detect the pitch's location long before it gets there, therefore improving his pitch selection — enabling him to use his areas strategically. Figure 2-9 shows a hitter using a reference point in the tunnel.

FIG 2-8. *Here the tunnel is shown from the viewpoint of the hitter. Notice how it starts out smaller and gradually gets larger.*

FIG 2-9. *Here a "tunneling hitter" understands the location of a pitch long before it reaches the strike zone.*

These reference points also have areas much like your strike zone, they have their own private rip areas and even areas. If the count is 2-and-0 and you're looking for a rip area fastball, you would be looking at the rip area in your fastball reference box, which connects the pitch to your rip area at the plate. This can be seen in Figure 2-10a.

Now, the curve ball has more of an arc and also has more downward and lateral movement; and because of this, the right-handed curve ball reference box will be higher and to the left of the fastball box. Figure 2-10b shows both the fastball and curve ball boxes and also how pitches coming through the off-centered curve ball box will end up in the strike zone. (For left-handers the box, of course, would be basically the same height but to the right.)

Also, the height placement of these boxes depends on the speed of the pitch. Though the boxes would be equal in size, a 90-mile-per-hour fastball would have its box lower than a 75-mile-per-hour fastball; and this is important to note. Figure 2-10c displays this idea.

After seeing a pitch one time in a game situation, a good hitter should be able to set up a reference box for that particular pitch. I feel that such boxes can and should be created for all pitches that follow a regular pattern; for example, fastballs, curves or sliders. However, a reference box will be useless against any pitch that tends to move in an irregular pattern. The best example of this type of pitch would be the knuckle ball.

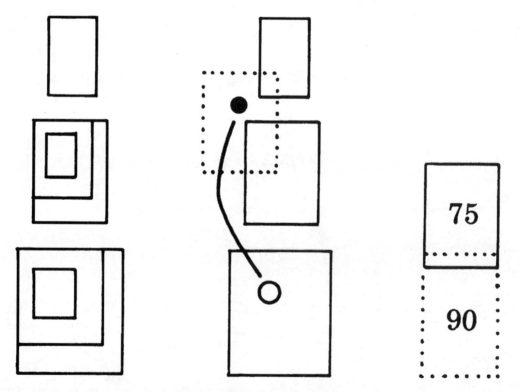

FIG 2-10 (a-c, left to right). *2-10a shows that the reference points, much like the strike zone, have their own connecting rip area and even area. 2-10b displays the different placement of a reference point when dealing with a breaking ball. 2-10c conveys the height difference as dictated by the speed of the pitch. One should note that the boxes in diagram (c) are placed to represent the ball at a point somewhere between mid and three-quarters way through flight.*

FIRST TIME UP

Closing out this section it is important to talk about your first at-bat in a game. Ted called the first at-bat the "key up." One of Ted's hard rules stated that before two strikes, if possible, a hitter should not swing at a pitch he has not yet seen go by. Ted believed that the first at-bat should be used by the hitter and team to gain information by making the pitcher pitch. I see the first at-bat in the same way with this addition —in theory, it is the most important and the most difficult at-bat of the day. In this at-bat the hitter is observing the speeds, the breaks, the look of the different pitches and their deliveries. With this information a hitter can make several timing notes, set his tunneling reference points and think about hitting the ball with authority.

Now somehow over the years the Ted Williams theory has been labeled as an approach suggesting a hitter should always take the first pitch, every at-bat. This is foolishness. One step further, these pitches in the first at-bat which we are observing don't necessarily have to be strikes. Let's walk through this so you can get the feel of what I mean.

You're on deck. You've seen the pitcher warm up three pitches — a fastball, a curve and a change-up. You get to the plate and here comes the fastball — average speed for your league. Pop. Ball one — just inside. Now in the time it takes for the catcher to return the ball to the pitcher and give new signs, you should do these following things:

1) Make some mental notes on the delivery, look and speed of the pitch you just saw.

2) Decide on the next probable pitch, in this case another fastball.

3) With the count and the pitcher's abilities in mind decide on the size of hitting area and therefore reference box — rip, even or the entire zone.

4) Visualize the box appropriately in the tunnel in relation to its speed and break (if it has a break).

In this case you are now prepared for an even area fastball. Here it comes. Fastball! But it is not through your reference box, rather it is away. You shut down. Pop. Strike one. It's right on the outside corner. Now at 1-and-1 you decide that the curve ball is the next probable pitch. But you hesitate. You have not seen the curve. Do you take a potential second strike for information's sake? Is gaining information worth a "two-strike at-bat?" Yes, it is. We are going to take that curve.

Now after reading the previous few lines you may very well be experiencing an example of what Lefty O'Doul was talking about. You are uncertain about taking this next pitch because you are afraid of creating a potential two-strike at-bat. But these feelings of anxiety are all due to a lack of knowledge. Here is the wisdom you are missing:

1) The true value of seeing a pitch before you go for it.

2) The average outcome that results when a hitter goes for pitches that he has not seen before.

3) The fact that two-strike hitting when approached well is no harder than regular hitting. It is just different — a different approach.

4) The fact that most curveballs that are taken at a 1-and-1 count are called balls and not strikes. At 1-and-1 the pitcher is up on you and he's not throwing any pitch down the middle.

So now you're back in there and you're taking. Here it comes — curve ball. But guess what? The hardest pitches to hit are the hardest pitches to throw and it's down low — ball two. Now we're at 2-and-1 and we've seen two of his three pitches. This is a good at-bat thus far and with each additional pitch your team's hungry hitters are watching — stalking the pitcher like lions in high grass. Even the ones that are not yet in the line-up.

Now, as with the fastball, you've made notes on the delivery, speed, break and general look of the curve. And you're glad you did, because from previous batters you are able to determine that at 2-and-1 he will most likely throw the curve again. You visually place your reference box in the tunnel and prepare for the curve in the even area. Here's the pitch. It's a curve — right through the reference box — you're swinging and... BOOM! A line drive to left center and a strong first at-bat. Look what you achieved — you have first-hand pitch information, the team has more pitch selection informa-tion, and as you take your lead off second base you know this pitcher has four less pitches to throw that day.

Here is what happens when I go to a high school game. The pitcher is warming up and only a couple of hitters are even watching. The first batter goes to the plate and swings at the first pitch — pop out to second. One down. I take a deep breath and let it out my nose. The second hitter takes a fastball. Ball one outside. He then takes another fastball right down the pipe. Now I'm starting to talk to myself a little... "Jesus kid, did you really think he was going to throw that curve? Three out of four hit the dirt in warm-ups. Whale that second fastball!" I glance over to the on-deck circle and there is an athletic-looking kid stretching out with his bat — getting loose but oblivious to the real matters at hand. Now here comes the curve and it is going to end up down but the kid bites at it while out over his front leg and nubs a ground ball to third. Two down. Now I'm looking for the concession stand...

FIG 2-11. *Coaching high school players can be difficult since there is so much going on in their lives. It is a tough time to take on the skill of hitting. When I coach these players I try and make it very clear to them what I want them to do and how I want them to do it. We then work together in accomplishing our team goals. I never let them off the hook and I feel that they respect me for that.*

The Swing Plane Mystery

How do you swing a bat at a baseball? Is it a down, level, or slight upswing? Studying this particular mystery off and on for eight years, I wish to share with you a most interesting conclusion. The swing plane mystery stems from an undiscovered piece of information — a corner ripped off the hitting treasure map. Hey, aren't most mysteries caused by a lack of information? In the movies they never tell you that the butler is the murder victim's real father or that the gardener is a CIA agent. This information doesn't come out until the end. When you finally piece the information together, you find that many prejudged factors are then seen in a different light.

Before I identify this missing link of swing plane information and hopefully solve the mystery it is important that we review the different types of swing planes as I have found them over the years. This review includes information gathered from the following sources: video tapes, books, newspaper articles, magazine articles, and coaches at the various levels of the game over the past twenty years.

FIG 3-1. *It would be nice if treasures had neat, easy-to-read maps that could lead you right to the bounty – but they don't. Maybe that's because the maps were written by pirates who often had one eye focused elsewhere... or maybe even pirates wanted treasure seekers to earn the prize themselves.*

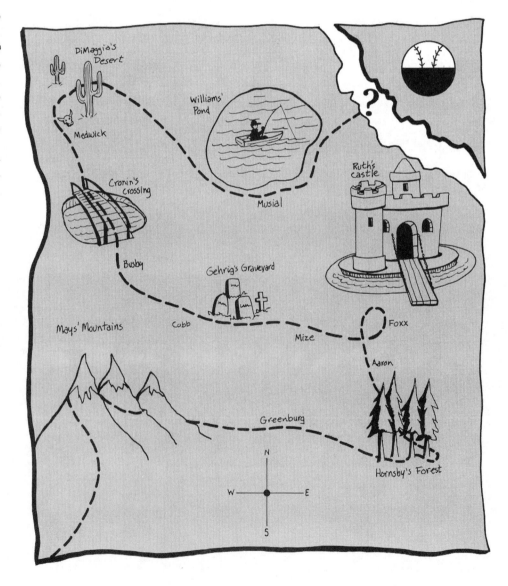

Looking first at the slight upswing, made popular by Ted in *The Science of Hitting,* we find a theory that basically states this: while the pitcher stands on a 10-inch mound and throws the ball from about ear level to an area around the hitter's knees, which most pitchers strive for, the ball is coming down. Therefore, if a hitter wishes to increase his contact percentages by having his bat stay within the path of the oncoming ball for the longest period of time, he must swing slightly up in relation to the ground; the swing thus level to the plane of the pitch. Figure 3-2 denotes the plane of this swing.

Most critics of the slight upswing will not dispute the idea of swinging slightly up to increase the chances of hitting a ball coming slightly down. However, most will begin criticizing the slight upswing as being ineffective. Coaches and players claim it is too big, that it is too long of a stroke and therefore it requires the talent of somebody like Ted Williams to handle it. After a short explanation of the slight upswing, Lau comments "My confidence in the accuracy of this theory is considerably undermined by the fact that I have never seen anyone make it work." Later he goes on to claim that not even Williams swung up. Lau and most attackers of the slight upswing will also claim that when it does work, it puts too many balls in the air. A ball hit into the air has come to be viewed by many over the years as the easiest place to field a ball. They'll be quick to say that if the ball is bouncing on the ground, often bouncing erratically, it's a harder ball to field. With the ball on the ground, the fielder has two jobs instead of one. He must field the ball and then still throw the runner out. Naturally, they conclude that balls hit on the ground can't help but lead to more errors, base runners, and runs scored.

FIG 3-2. *The slight upswing travels slightly up in relation to the ground. It travels on the same plane as the pitch which is traveling slightly down upon release from the pitcher atop the mound.*

Another popular attack made on the slight upswing is that it is not feasible for the fast runner — the guy who can fly down the line, the argument being that most of the runner's game is on the ground, with grounders up the middle and through the holes. Why should this hitter ever want to use an air-plagued slight upswing? They often summarize that the slight upswing is a swing only good for power hitters.

What about down and then up? Sometimes you will hear hitters claim that they swing down and then up. While it sounds odd, there is a lot of truth to the claim and we will discuss this in a moment. For our purposes, those hitters are categorized as slight up-plane hitters. While they start down, their intention is to have their bats traveling slightly upward during any potential contact with the ball.

Hopping planes to the downswing, this hitter is swinging down in relation to both the oncoming plane of the ball and the ground. Figure 3-3 illustrates this swing. The major support of this theory is built not only upon the advantages of hitting the ball on the ground, but also on the idea that the downswing will very rarely, if at all, produce an easy-to-field pop-up or fly ball. Advocates of the downswing will claim that when it's executed properly it will produce both hard grounders and line drives. Downswing defendants also claim that balls hit off a downswing will possess an aiding backspin, causing line drives to carry farther than when hit with either of the two competing strokes. Figure 3-4 displays this spin.

Critics of the downswing will attack its very small potential contact area, claiming that its use cuts down the percentages of any type of contact — good or bad. As far as ground balls go, most will agree that the grounder can be a more difficult play; however, most do not believe that hitting the majority of your balls on the ground is a strong foundation for success. Critics will claim that the power hitter usually has no game on the ground, due to their usual size and speed. They then ask, "Why would the power hitter use a swing plagued with ground balls?" Some critics simply ask, "How many doubles have you ever seen hit on the ground?"

The last and certainly the most popular of the three theories is the level swing. Before we review the level swing, however, please note that when I speak of level, I am referring to a swing traveling on a plane level to the ground as illustrated in Figure 3-5. While the majority of level swing supporters define their swing as level to the ground, a small minority of them

FIG 3-3 & 3-4 (inset). *The downswing travels down in relation to the ground. This stroke tends to cut the ball and create backspin.*

FIG 3-5. *The level swing travels level in relation to the ground. It is by far the most popular stroke in baseball, but that statistic doesn't necessarily prove this approach is best.*

will confusingly claim their swing is traveling on a plane level to the ball, therefore, in my mind, they then become slight upswing supporters.

Followers of the level swing build their case upon one major point — that the level swing will aid the hitter in hitting the center of the ball and a resulting line drive more often than the other two theories. Level swingers usually view the slightly upswings and downswings as opposite extremes, protesting that both are infested with an abundance of off-centered contact, this of course causing the bat to hit either the top half of the ball in the downswing for a harvest of grounders, or the bottom half in the slight upswing for a herd of pops and flies.

Interesting in itself is that unlike the other theories, most level swing people believe their swing is the ideal swing, that is, the swing for all hitters regardless of style. They'll claim the level swing produces not only a reasonable percentage of fly balls for the power hitter, but also a reasonable percentage of ground balls for the runner.

Arguments against the level swing are not in abundance. Again, it is the most popular swing. However, slight upswing believers, as you might suspect, will claim that it could have a better potential contact zone. Those who promote the downswing will say it produces "too many balls in the air," and point out the absence of that beneficial backspin we spoke of. Still the question remains, *"On which plane will your career ride?"*

The missing clue to the swing plane mystery is what I call the lighting effect. You see, regardless of when or where you hit, the light is always above. Whether it's a sunny day, a cloudy day, an indoor batting cage or a night game, the light is always coming down. The result is a pitch where the top of the ball is brighter than the bottom. Because the light is coming down on a non-transparent sphere, the bottom does not have the angle to pick up as much light and therefore it is darker. It's in the shade! Also, keep in mind that the hitter is looking down on the pitch. Most pitches are thrown at knee level and rarely in the vicinity of the eyes.

What does this have to do with the plane of the swing? Unfortunately, even at the slowest speeds, where the two tones are easily detected, the top of the ball is more attractive to the hitter. In the split-second high-pressured skill of hitting, the top of the ball lures the hitter to attack it rather than the ball's center. Going a step further, when we increase the velocity to 80 or 90 miles an hour, the bottom of the ball can be impossible to see. At a high speed the lighting effect displays the top of the ball like a neon sign, catching both the hitter's attention and attack. Have you ever heard a hitter say that a pitcher was throwing seeds, pills or BB's? What they were experiencing was the optical illusion of the ball becoming smaller, when in reality it had only changed size in relation to their ability to see it in its entirety. Due to the lighting effect, hitters are only seeing and hitting the top half of the ball, as seen in Figure 3-6.

When I was a young coach at the Ted Williams Camp, Ted sat down to dinner with me and a couple of other young coaches. He said, "You know Ferroli, I went to the plate 7706 times in my career and every time I tried to get the ball in the air!" Then in a puzzled, questioning kind of way he said, "But I still made more outs on the ground!" I then respectfully explained my theory of the lighting effect and I will always believe that it was this conversation that captured his interest in me.

FIG 3-6. *Because the lighting source originates from above, the top of the ball is brighter than the bottom half. This subtle detail has a major effect on the plane of the swing.*

If all hitters have been attacking the top half of the ball while under the impression that they are attacking the entire ball, it makes sense that the most productive and popular swing plane would be the one that has brought the bat to the center of the ball regardless of what the hitter sees, thinks or how he attacks. The level swing has generally been viewed as the proper plane, the best way to bring the bat and the hitter to the center of the ball. Remember, however, it has done so while the hitter is attacking the wrong target! Therefore, the success and popularity of the level swing has rested upon the odd fact that the downward plane of the pitch coupled with the plane of the level swing creates a tendency for contact to be made below the target the hitter means to attack.

I'm hoping you can get the same chuckle out of all this as I have. Due to a legitimate optical illusion, the hitter has been mistakenly attacking the wrong part of the ball for as long as there has been light. The level swing, by way of *geometric coincidence*, has done a great job correcting his mistake. What's funny is that all this has gone on literally under the hitter's nose without him knowing it.

You should find it interesting that the level swing will only bring a hitter to the center of the ball when the ball is coming down! Hypothetically, the hitter, using a level swing to contact a level pitch, would probably ground it out because now the aiding angular relation between the path of the pitch and the path of the swing would not bring his contact point on the ball below the original target. Remember, this hitter does not realize he is attacking the top of the ball. This hitter believes he is seeing a complete ball that looks small because it's going fast. These concepts can be seen in Figures 3-7 and 3-8.

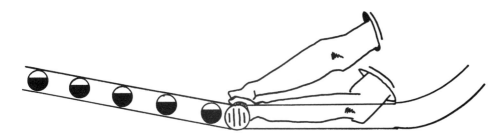

FIG 3-7. *"Unaware" of the lighting effect, the level swing has "found" the center of the ball traveling "down."*

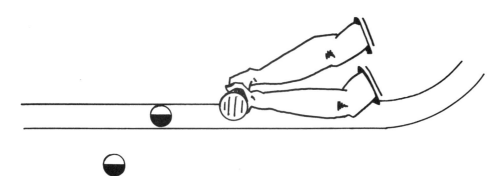

FIG 3-8. *"Unaware" of the lighting effect, the level swinger would "ironically ground out" the level pitch.*

Now that the hitter understands that the top of the ball is brighter than the bottom, there is no need to rely on coincidence for the bat to attack the center of the ball. The hitter should adjust his target area to *under the white*. In other words, whatever he sees he should think about aiming slightly under it. Not a ton! Just a hair under the white. Then adjust the swing plane to *slightly up*! Absolutely...positively...slightly up!

Once a hitter understands how the lighting effect hides the center of the ball, he would be foolish not to take advantage of the potential contact area created by the slight upswing. If you take a good look at Figures 3-9 and 3-10 and notice the amount of time that the bat is in the potential contact area in comparison to its competition, it is hard to believe that anybody would swing any other way. The slight upswing

allows the hitter the greatest range of error. You can be a little late or a little early and still get a good piece of the ball.

Also, a hitter not swinging slightly up is cutting himself short by not using the only swing that is designed to hit the ball right smack on the nose. In the level swing the ball gets cut — you know, sliced. It's cut even more so in the downswing. The slight upswing drives the ball, however. On the average the slight upswing produces much more push or drive than spin or cut. These concepts can be seen further in Figure 3-10.

As for the argument that the slight upswing puts too many balls in the air, that simply isn't true. Before my study of the lighting effect, I found it, just as Ted did, to be more ground ball prone. It's really simple to figure out. Though

FIG 3-9. *A slight upswing that aims "under the white" will render the best contact for all types of hitters.*

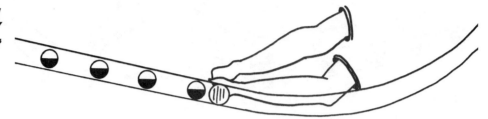

FIG 3-10. *The slight upswing keeps the bat in the potential contact zone for the greatest period of time and therefore offers the hitter a greater margin of timing error. It also results in a ball that is struck square as opposed to cut with a slice (a ball hit on both the other planes – the downswing plane and the level swing plane – result in a slice at contact).*

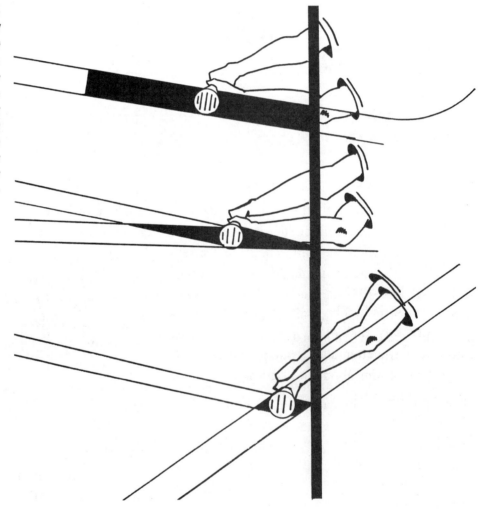

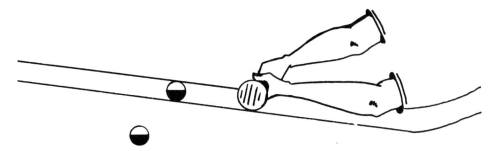

FIG 3-11. *Much like a level swinger at a level pitch, the slight upswinger, unaware of the lighting effect, will ground out the ball that's traveling down.*

the plane of the swing was in line with the plane of the pitch, the target was still the top of the ball. The result, much like the level swing at the level pitch, is a ground ball. This is seen in Figure 3-11.

Also, the slight upswing is geared toward hitting line drives. If you imagine a ball hit from your belt buckle back through the pitcher's release point, that ball is going to be a line drive. Remember, the slight upswing is based on meeting the plane of the bat with the average plane of the ball. If the ball comes in at 8 to 10 degrees, good execution will send it back out on that same angle.

As for the downswing, I think it's foolishness because it barely has a potential contact area. Anybody that hits well swinging down could be way better than what they are. I will support the claim about the ball spinning and carrying. Sliced balls have a backspin and will carry, but they won't carry farther than a ball hit on the nose. There is no comparison. Cut, line drives that are hit with downswings hang in the air, making them easier to field. A hard line drive to field is one with a topspin sliced off the slight upswing, because it will sink; or even worse, if you hit it right on the nose, it will knuckle.

As a matter of fact, if you slice or cut *just under* a line drive, using the slight upswing, it often ends up of over the fence.

What about the question of slightly up being a longer stroke? I can't argue to much with that. I think it is a longer stroke, but its quality result is worth the time. Do you want a sit-down dinner or drive-through? In a moment, I'm going to show you a system for cutting the length of stroke considerably. But until then, I have to say that without question, most critics of the slight up plane do not understand the basics of *timing*. Therefore, the longer stroke becomes more difficult for them to handle. When they fail, they then perceive the main problem to be length of stroke because that is all they understand. In reality that is not the problem at all. They have judged the stroke after using it incorrectly.

While we're on the subject, do you see the ball better on a bright day or a gray day? Good question, isn't it? I pondered over this one for a long while and concluded that a bright day, a sunny day, was far better. After I realized that the top half of the ball was brighter, the next logical question to ask was this — "Is the top half of the ball brighter on a sunny day than on a gray day? Naturally, the answer is yes. I feel

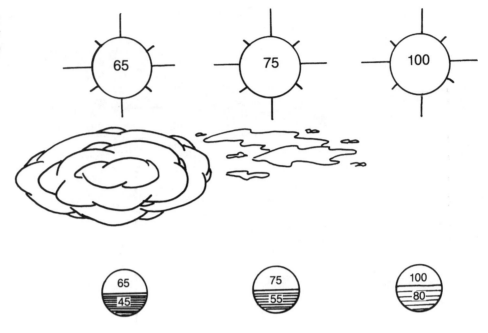

the best way to think of lighting is like reading a book under different watt bulbs. The brighter the bulb, the clearer the print. The brighter the day, the clearer the ball, therefore making it easier to see and easier to hit. This is displayed in Figure 3-12.

I know. You want to know what to aim for if you're playing a game and the sun is setting, causing its light to shine from the side, as seen in Figure 3-13. Well, aim for the white, because in this case the ball's height, the key dimension in target area, is represented truly.

You may have noticed that I did not identify the uppercuts as a seeing plane. We all know what it is, but it is never taught. I've never heard anyone say, "My players uppercut." As you may figure. I don't believe in it. If baseball does not view it as a popular swing plane, I certainly don't want to get anybody considering it. Mo Vaughn of the Red Sox uppercuts and I'm sure he does so to get the ball up in the air — to be a power hitter. But, he would be better off slightly up while aiming under the white.

One of the problems in hitting a baseball is the misconception that there is a relationship between the style of hitter and the swing plane. This is a fallacy. Do all hitters hit the same way? No! And I'll lay out those differences later. But until they dig a big hole and place the mound five feet below ground level, I'll say all hitters swing slightly up.

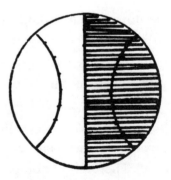

FIG 3-13. *Sometimes, the sun will be setting and the ball will appear as is shown above. In this case, the height of the ball is represented truly, so aim for the white.*

40

The Moves Of The Hitter

Like life itself, in hitting time is the most valuable thing you can have. Everything you do will be done to give you more time; whether we're talking about stance, the weight of the bat, position in the batter's box, length of stride, or the shifting of the weight, the bottom line is time. The more time you have, the better. Ted calls this the heart of hitting. He will say, *"The more time you have, the less chance you have of being fooled."* Remember, if that ball is traveling at 90 miles per hour, it will get there in about four-tenths of a second; you'd better have time or it's going by you. I have learned that time at the plate is developed by solidifying certain mechanics in the swing. These mechanics work together to not only give you more time, but also the power you need to hit the ball hard and with consistency.

FIG 4-1. *Everything we do in hitting is in the effort to gain more time. At ninety miles an hour a pitch will travel from the release point to the plate in about four-tenths of a second.*

It is important at this point to note that the movements in hitting are intertwined so that they both rely on and affect one another. Therefore, all of the following mechanics will be equally important when trying to develop a good swing. Because of this, I suggest you carefully examine and attempt all of the mechanics I present, noticing not just their individual worth, but their dependence on one another.

Before we talk about the hitter's movements we must take a look at his stance. While I agree that everybody has their own personal stance, I also know that a good stance must have certain ingredients. Your stance is important because it is your starting point. In a sense, it is your first hitting movement! I mean, you didn't get up this morning in your stance — you moved to get in it. Your stance should be designed or altered to help you hit.

I like to see a hitter with his knees and waist slightly bent; his feet should be about shoulder width apart, with the front foot slightly open and the back foot straight across. The body weight is evenly distributed, not forward on the front foot or back on the back foot. The stance is balanced, with the weight falling through the center of the body, and both arms are bent at each elbow joint.

The height of the hands should be as close to the middle of the strike zone as possible and relatively close to the body, about three to eight inches away. The body is comfortable; the midsection untwisted, with the head straight up and the eyes level. The hitter's feet are flat on the ground, providing a stable base. The hitter's body is as relaxed as possible.

Okay, bubble gum and sunflower seeds at arm's length? Pride and ego all warmed up? Let's talk about the movements of the hitter — his mechanics.

THE PRE-SWING (THE COCK-ING MOTION AND STRETCH POSITION)

The first phase of movement is the phase that prepares the hitter to hit the probable pitch with both consistency and authority. I call this movement phase the *pre-swing*. Ted referred to hitting as a pendulum — a movement back, followed by a movement forward, "a move and counter move." The first movements of the pre-swing, what I call the *cocking motion*, represent the hitter's backward flow of that pendulum. The cocking motion begins before the stride about the time the pitcher starts to break his hands in his wind-up. It is executed by bending the back knee straight down and the front knee in and down at the same time. These body movements should be smooth and comfortable, like a pitcher's motion. The bending of the two knees will cause the body not only to shift its weight more onto the back leg, but also to twist in towards the plate. These movements can be seen in Figure 4-2 (a-b).

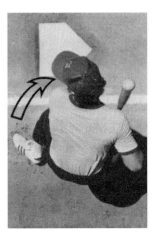

FIG 4-3 (a-b, left to right). *Photo sequence (a-b) shows how the heel lifts as the front foot rolls onto the outside of its big toe.*

During the cocking motion the heel of the front foot will lift, causing the foot to roll up onto the outside of its big toe. While this is happening, however, the angle that the front foot was on in the stance (slightly open) will not change. This can be seen in Figure 4-3 (a-b).

Also the hitter should note that in the cocking motion, his entire body will lean into the plate just slightly. This is accomplished by the hitter coming onto the ball of his back foot from a flat-footed stance.

Looking at the top of the hitter, his eyes will not leave sight of the pitcher, with the head as still as possible. Also, as the body flows back, the hitter should think about his front shoulder turning in and down, much like his front knee. This is important. The hitter must note that the stance angle of the front foot and the hitter's complete vision of the pitcher should control the extent of the backward rotation. If the front toe rotates back toward the catcher like the front knee and shoulder, the original stance angle of the foot will be destroyed and the hitter will have rotated back too far. The same will hold true if the hitter's nose blocks the back eye's sight of

FIG 4-2 (a-b, left to right). *Photo sequence (a-b) displays "the cocking motion." It is achieved by bending the back knee straight down and the front knee in and down at the same time.*

the pitcher. If you cock back with your front eye closed and find your nose slightly in your view, you are rotating back too much.

If I had to pick one movement of a hitter's mechanics that I considered to be the most important, it would be the second move of the pre-swing — the *stretch position*. That's because the stretch position is not only responsible for placing the body in a position of potential speed and power, but it is also where the hitter starts his counter move forward — it's where he gets his body going. Smoothly following the cocking motion and when the pitcher's arm is over his throwing shoulder, the hitter will twist into the stretch position by striding and opening his front foot while trying to rotate his front shoulder for the second time back toward the catcher.

Although the hitter is making one movement by rotating his hips forward with his stride and another separate movement by making an additional attempt (besides the cocking motion) to rotate the upper body back, these movements are occurring in unison and therefore I consider them to be components of one large parting movement. Remember, the hitter is rotating his upper body and lower body in different directions at the same time as he strides forward.

Figure 4-4 (a-b) show these opposite lower and upper body movements to the stretch position. Notice after the cocking motion how the front toe is opening out, while the front heel travels only a short distance. Also notice how the upper body turns back at the same time, while the arms remain relatively still. Why are these movements so important?

By rotating the upper body and lower body in different directions, we are stretching the muscles that indirectly connect these segments; and as a result, connecting them directly together. That is to say, that we are preparing or

FIG 4-4 (a-b, left to right). *Photo sequence (a-b) shows what may be the most important mechanical move of the hitter. After the hitter cocks back, the hips and shoulders must separate during the flight of the stride.*

positioning the body in such a way that when the lower body begins to rotate forward, it will immediately pull the upper body behind it.

Before we observe the results of the stretch position in an actual swing sequence, let us first see the same concept displayed with the simple illustrations shown in Figure 4-5.

Example (A) presents two toy train pieces: an engine and a boxcar. As you can see, these pieces are connected by a rubber band that lies with slack between them. Naturally, the engine is much heavier than the boxcar and, unlike the boxcar, possesses the ability to pull things. Now, if the engine was started and driven slowly to the left, while at the exact same time the boxcar was shoved once, making it move slowly to the right, the rubber band would begin to stretch, As the rubber band continued to stretch to its limit, both the engine and boxcar would slow down. However, because the boxcar is lighter and lacks a continual source of drive, it would eventually stop, and get pulled in the opposite direction by the engine, as indicated by Examples (B) and (C).

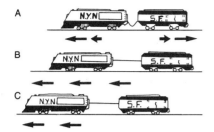

FIG 4-5. *Only when the slack between engine and boxcar has been taken up will the engine begin to exert power and tow the box car.*

Whether it's a hitter's upper body and lower body, or two pieces of a toy train, when we move them apart we are preparing the muscle, or elastic, between them to tow the lighter piece, the upper body, or the boxcar, directly without any slack. Therefore, we now tow the object without delay. The effect of the stretch position on an actual swing becomes vivid when the following swing sequences are compared.

The first photo sequence, Figure 4-6 (a-c), relays a swing launched from the stretch position. Notice after the cocking motion how the front knee and front shoulder have traveled apart, insuring a good stretch position and deleting any possible slack between the two. Also notice how, after the decision to swing is made, the lower body and upper body respond at the same time. Because the upper body and lower body were set apart in the stretch position, they now move as one unit, no different than the two train pieces. When the lower body rotates, the upper body must follow.

On the contrary, Figure 4-7 (a-c) demonstrates a swing that has been launched from a poor pre-swing — a pre-swing that had neglected to form the stretch position. Notice after the cocking motion how only the front foot and hips begin to open, while the front shoul-

FIG 4-6 (a-c, left to right). *From the stretch position there is no lag time between the lower and upper body as shown in photo sequence (a-c).*

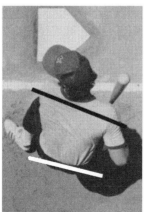  

FIG 4-7 (a-c, left to right). *Without the stretch position time is lost before the upper body responds as shown in photo sequence (a-c).*

der remains stationary, therefore overlooking the parting movement necessary for deleting the slack. Notice how the hips are free to open after a decision to swing without any coupling to the upper body and therefore the bat. Also, pay particular notice to the time that has passed on the clock before the response of the upper body. The conclusion here will be an old story by the end of this book; it's the loss of time and power due to incorrect movement or preparation.

If we take two hitters, all things being equal except the utilization of the stretch position, the hitter who executes it properly will be much quicker. The no-slack connection of the upper body and lower body will force his upper body and bat response to be immediate, therefore enabling him to view the ball longer before he must commit his swing. This hitter has more time and therefore will see the ball longer and receive clearer information, resulting in better pitch selection and a cut-down of times when he would have been fooled.

On the other hand, the hitter who does not prepare properly will swing with an unnecessary delay — a lag time between body segments. This hitter sees every pitch seemingly faster than it is and must commit himself earlier to make up for his slower swing. This hitter does not see the ball as long before his swing and is forced

to condense his information. Naturally, he must make rushed decisions, causing him to be fooled more often by both the type of pitch and overall location. It's interesting to note how a neglect of mechanical execution can cause mental breakdowns.

Neglect of the stretch position results in another loss — power. Now, when I say power, please don't misunderstand me; I don't necessarily mean long balls. I mean power in relation to your style — in relation to your personal potential. Looking at the swing with power in mind, the lower body and upper body represent the swing's two greatest sources of momentum; and without proper execution of the stretch position, these two sources of momentum will be used separately and consequently inadequately. For the power potential to be realized the swing must start with the lower body directly pulling the upper body behind it. The baseball swing is a kinetic chain — a full body gyration.

For a practical example of this concept, let's say you and your friend have been hired to knock down a wall, and to do the job you rent two identical bulldozers. After you fire them up you each take a shot, one by one, at ramming the wall, but the wall won't fall. After coffee, your friend says, "Let's drive them into the wall at the same time." Boom! Down it comes, a job well done ... I'm sure you can see what I'm getting at. Every hitter has two bulldozers — two major weight areas that contribute to creating the hitter's swing momentum. These areas are the upper and lower bodies. And the only way a hitter can tap their combined momentum potential is by driving them together from the stretch position. The baseball "swing" is a full body movement that funnels its momentum down to the point of contact. Naturally, we want all the momentum available.

Don't Forget the Importance of the Stretch Position!!

Due to the importance of the stretch position, it's important to check its quality periodically. This can be done by having the hitter freeze after he lands his stride, and then while holding this position the hitter searches for the feeling of slight tension in certain areas. If a hitter does not feel any tension in these areas, something may be out of sync and he best review. In Figures 4-8 and 4-9 we see the stretch position with a labeling of these common tension areas. Please note, however, that these tensions will go unnoticed in an actual swing due to the short space of time in which the muscles are stretched.

LANDING AND HIP ROTATION

Like Ted, I've found that hip rotation is the true root of batting speed and power. However, to acquire good hip rotation the hitter must learn to use both his legs and weight properly. Again, proper execution demands good preliminary positioning, and here we are setting the stage for good rotation by landing the front leg correctly after the stride.

During the flight period of the stride, the front knee and foot will remain in the same position that they assumed in the cocking motion. The only front leg movement is an outward rotation of the leg from the front hip. Figure 4-10 (a-b) shows the stride from the cocking motion. Notice how it then lands in that same position, with the toe touching down first and the knee still bent.

FIG 4-8 & 4-9 (top to bottom). *The stretch position can be checked by freezing it and noting the feeling of slight tension behind the neck, in the lower back, inside the front leg, and behind the shoulders.*

FIG 4-10 (a-b, left to right). *Photo sequence (a-b) conveys how the front leg "opens" in a fixed position and lands that way with the toe touching down first.*

FIG 4-11 (a-b, left to right). *Photo sequence (a-b) shows how the stride brings the hitter to a balanced position – a position where his weight is evenly distributed.*

FIG 4-12. *Notice how the front foot lands on the inside of the big toe. The pressure is felt at the "base" of that toe.*

Another very important element of landing is *balance*. When the hitter lands that stride foot correctly, he should feel his body weight follow to a point of balance. That is to say the hitter's weight again becomes evenly distributed between the front and back feet, like in his stance. This can be seen in Figure 4-11 (a-b).

Notice how the upper body eventually becomes situated in between the front and back feet, with the front shoulder slightly down. Also notice in Figure 4-12 how the foot lands on the inside of the big toe. (Actually, the pressure is at the base of the toe, not at the top.) Assuming

that the pitch is timed correctly, a hitter landing properly will be at the peak of his physical preparation. What happens next?

If the hitter chooses to let the ball go by, the pendulum movement will stop when the hitter lands. However, if he decides to swing, the pendulum will continue harmoniously into the rotation of his hips. As you can see in Figure 4-13 (a-d), when the hitter decides to swing from a position where his weight is evenly distributed from leg to leg, the bent front leg begins to extend, begins to straighten out, therefore pushing the front hip back and around the corner

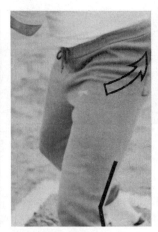

FIG 4-13 (a-d, left to right). *Photo sequence (a-d) illustrates that only a front leg that is straightening can push the front hip back. This can only start from a leg that has landed in a bent position.*

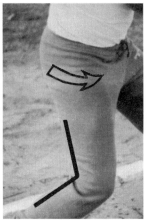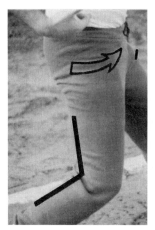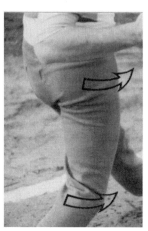

FIG 4-14 (a-d, left to right). *Photo sequence (a-d) shows that only the rotation of a "bent back leg" will thrust the back hip forward on the proper plane.*

towards the catcher. Meanwhile, at the exact same time the back leg, which has also remained bent from the cocking motion, pivots on the ball of its foot. Due to its bent position, this thrusts the back hip forward and around its corner as seen in Figure 4-14 (a-d).

Good technique demands two separate forces at opposite ends of the lever, pushing in unison in opposite directions. The result is a pinwheel-type movement — rotation of the hips by both legs. Figure 4-15 shows the concept.

Note that if the front leg had not landed correctly after the stride — if it had reached out,

as in Figure 4-16, extending the knee prematurely, the front hip would be left with no power source to push it. Now the hitter would have to rely solely on the rotation of the bent back leg, which is just not enough. Hitters who reach out their stride leg by extending their stride knee prematurely are left with less momentum when it comes time to hit because they have eliminated a power source. It's much like asking someone to hop without first bending their knee. This is another reason why that front knee must turn in during the cocking motion. The hitter is bending it more to be used later in the swing.

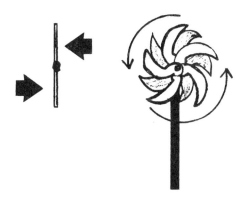

FIG 4-15. *Hip rotation is a pinwheel effect caused by the legs pushing each hip in unison.*

FIG 4-16. *Here the hitter's front knee has reached out prematurely. The result – the hitter is left with no "power source" by which to push the front hip. This is extremely important since the front leg is the stronger source of power of the two legs.*

Similar is the preparation and use of the back leg. If the knee of the back leg is not bent at least in the stance, the back hip will not thrust forward because its power source is a pivoting bent back leg. If that leg is not bent the hitter depends solely on the front leg for rotation, and again, that's not enough. Good hip rotation depends on proper use of the legs for support.

Considering the task involved, along with how the hips and legs are connected, to start hip rotation the weight must be evenly distributed on both legs. If the weight remains too far back or comes too far forward, there will be too much weight on the back or front leg, slowing down and restricting its movement.

Balance is one of my arguments against the Charlie Lau theory. In *The Art of Hitting .300*, Lau states and lists in his "Absolutes of Good Hitting", that you hit over your front foot. Naturally, I disagree. The swing starts between both feet because this is the position in which the hitter can begin the strongest and quickest rotation. Ironically, as the body rotates, the axis tilts back just slightly. This can be seen in Figure 4-17 (a-b). The ideal baseball swing starts off both legs and then favors the back leg.

FIG 4-18. *Here the hitter's front foot is closed (though more open than suggested in the Lau theory) and the hitter's hips are restricted while the upper body continues.*

Think about it. If you were to continue coming forward to hit off your front leg (which used to be called lunging), you would undoubtedly run into problems (Figure 4-18). This is demonstrated from cover to cover in Lau's book by George Brett, who in my opinion had a very well-balanced swing in real life. First of all, you would immediately become slower with the bat and cut down your reaction time because now your average contact point would be much closer to the pitcher's release point.

Comparing Figures 4-19 (a-c), we find a difference of about three feet! Have you ever hit a ball at the label? I know you've hit a few on the fat part. The way I see it, the label is an out and the fat part is success. How far are those two points away from each other on the bat? Not very far. So why give the pitcher a three foot advantage when just a little can slaughter you?

You won't get good hip rotation off the front foot — you can't! When your weight is over your front leg your cleat will grip tight in the dirt and that front leg is just not going to open. Sure, I've seen those hitters who seem to possess the ability to spin their hips around while their front foot is cemented in the dirt, but that's unnatural

FIG 4-17 (a-b, left to right). *Photo sequence (a-b) illustrates the use of "both legs" during the swing. The ideal swing should utilize "both legs" and favor the "back leg" at contact.*

FIG 4-19 (a-c, left to right). *From the starting point marked by an arrow in 4-19a, we see a comparison of the Williams and Lau approach. 4-19b displays contact with a high fastball according to the Williams theory. 4-19c shows the same pitch with the Lau theory contacted much closer to the pitcher. The three arrows in 4-19c allow a comparison of the two different contact points in relation to starting point.*

and certainly not very healthy. To me it's more like something Moe would do to torture Larry. I'll tell you right now the average guy can't move like that — not to the extent that is necessary. If you base part of your success on something that's anatomically unnatural, I don't think you're off to a very good start.

Certainly hitting off the front foot makes seeing the ball much more difficult because, as you come onto the front leg, your eyes have got to come up. I've known front-foot hitters to come back to the bench claiming the pitcher has a great sinker. So I'd get up and, sure enough, no sinker. Hey, it's simple — the eyes go up, the ball appears to go down. As I got older, to avoid 20-minute conversations during games, I learned to say, "Yeah, good sinker."

There's another factor, too. When you come that far forward, you're coming too far forward with your head and eyes. You've created two timing variables — not only is the ball coming at you, but you're coming at the ball as well. If I threw 500 tennis balls at you while you were standing still and then 500 more when you were jogging toward me, in which situation would you be more successful? Standing still, of course, so why try and time two things instead of one? It makes no sense. All hitters must come forward slightly, but not to this degree.

The low ball is definitely harder to hit off your front leg because your eyes are further away and you have to reach more. Viewing Figure 4-20 (a-b) you can see how much closer my eyes are to the ball when swinging with balance. Does Lau list a little extra hand-eye coordination as an absolute of good hitting? He should because you'll need it if your eyes are farther away or moving up.

Hey, I'm not saying a ball can't be hit hard by coming onto the front leg, it's really like a golf swing; and there is plenty of momentum. But in hitting, unlike in golf, it is impractical because there is a timing factor. A golf ball is not moving at you. You don't have to catch it at a specific point out of the air, you just have to

FIG 4-20 (a-b, left to right). *Photo sequence (a-b) illustrates how front-foot hitting not only causes the eyes to rise, but also takes them further away from the contact point.*

hit it. In golf, momentum can be created by lunging forward. In baseball, it must be generated from a circular pattern. What people forget when they talk about swinging and power is the actual task at hand. Swinging for maximum power and hitting are two different worlds! I'm not writing a book about how to hit a baseball as hard as you can, and neither did Ted. We have written books about hitting balls as hard and as often as possible. Ted's technique observes and caters to both power and timing combined. Lau's front foot swing is inferior in view of the task.

Why do people use it? It's easier. The Lau swing is an easier swing to learn. Unfortunately, as its followers climb the baseball ladder, they may very well wish they worked harder and followed logic, because while the Lau swing is easy to learn, it's much harder to hit with. Sure, the Williams stroke requires some work, but so does everything else that's worthwhile. Certainly it's not that hard. This swing is no more difficult to learn than shooting a basketball. It's merely good instruction and practice. Figures 4-21 (a-d) and 4-22 (a-d) demonstrate the two strokes.

FIG 4-21 (a-d, left to right). *Photo sequence (a-d) illustrates "front-foot hitting." Actually, in accordance with the Lau theory, my front foot has again "opened" too much.*

FIG 4-22 (a-d, left to right). *Photo sequence (a-d) outlines a swing that starts from a balanced position and then favors the back foot.*

LANDING THE SLIGHT UP PLANE

Ten years ago in *Disciple of a Master* I identified a phase of hitting called the dip phase. I said it was the beginning of the swing — the very next move after the stretch position where the legs and hips start to pull everything through hard. Obviously, if we are going to swing slightly up, the back shoulder and barrel of the bat must drop down and under so they can then come up. This is the dip phase. Therefore the old saying; "Don't drop the back shoulder" is not true. Figure 4-23 (a-b) display the point of the swing I was talking about.

Today on the tube or attending a local game, I am very pleased to see so many solid stretch positions and dip phases. Fifteen years ago very few players made these movements at any level of baseball and to me it clearly shows progress in hitting approach. Hoping to continue this progress I am going to identify a more efficient way to launch the slight upswing. (This is the shortening of the stroke I referred to earlier.)

Here we will create a new landing position by merging the dip phase with the stretch position. As the hitter strides forward the following things will happen before his foot hits the ground. The batter will separate the upper and lower body to obtain the stretch position. He will have leveled off the bat. He will drop the back shoulder and allow the front shoulder and elbow to ride up. This is shown in Figure 4-24 (a-b).

Notice how the front knee is still bent as the hitter lands. Look at the back knee, also still bent, but now with a slight rotation. Note the lift of the back heel. Notice that the hips and upper body are much further along in their rotation. Look at the height and position of the hands. The bat's barrel, now already low, awaits the start of the slight upswing. Notice the position of the backside elbow in relation to its hip.

FIG 4-23 (a-b, top to bottom). *Photo sequence (a-b) shows the dip phase as the starting point of a swing where (after landing) the hitter drops the back shoulder with the beginning of hip rotation.*

FIG 4-24 (a-b, left to right). *Photo sequence (a-b) shows a new landing position which merges the stretch position with the dip phase.*

LANDING A   **LANDING B**

FIG 4-25 (a-b, left to right). *Photo sequence (a-b) displays the side view of two very different landings. Both pictures were shot as the front foot touches down – they both apear balanced and loaded.*

LANDING A   **LANDING B**

FIG 4-26 (a-b, left to right). *Photo sequence (a-b) features the two landings but display their rotating relationship to the landing point. Keep in mind that the front foot has just touched down at this point in the swing.*

What makes this a more efficient landing position? Looking at Figure 4-25 (a-b) we can compare the two different landings. First and foremost landing A puts the torso, arms, hands and bat in a much better position to swing slightly up. Look at the shoulder line and hip line. They are slanting up. Notice the bat's barrel in landing A. It is down. It is just waiting to rocket slightly up and head on into the pitch.

Now look at landing B, the more upright and customary landing position. The shoulder line is flat. The hip line is flat. Look at the barrel of the bat. It is much further away from potential contact. In order to swing slightly up this hitter must drop the back shoulder and bring the bat down and under. He has to make a big loop taking up more time.

Landing A has created a shorter stroke in a circular way. A slight rotation of the hips during the stride has brought the barrel of the bat much closer to the average contact point. In Figure 4-26 (a-b) look at the relationship of the hips and bat to the potential contact area from landing A. Now view the same in landing B. The

bat and hips are much further away. (It is important that you note how I am linking length of stroke to a rotation of the hips.) From landing B the hitter has to travel much further to contact.

Finally, landing A has accomplished all of the above, before a decision to swing! While landing B must now execute all of the above, after a decision to swing. By combining two steps, the dip and the stretch, we have saved a whole step and therefore valuable time. From landing A the hitter will have less to do after a swing decision.

Now, I am not saying that landing B should be eliminated from baseball. I just want you to clearly understand the choices. Landing B has the stretch position. It is balanced and it has plenty of power. It is also fairly easy to learn and maintain. Landing A is more advanced. Its balance and stretch are more complex (will elaborate). Its movements are not as easy to learn. But landing A without question is an easier position to hit from. In the spirit of progress I have outlined it for you.

Think about it. What is at the beginning of slightly up? It's slightly down! And that is where landing A puts the bat and the back half of the body. It places the hitter at the beginning of the slight upswing.

Before we go on, I want to make a point about the balance of these two landings. When I use the term balance, I mean weight distributed evenly between the back and front foot. I'm concerned with balance in the direction of the pendulum. Without going into it more than necessary, if you're landing either of these forms correctly, you should be able to check them simply with the pressure of a fair push. A well balanced landing will stay balanced against a push on either the front shoulder back or the back shoulder forward. This is illustrated in Figure 4-27 (a-b).

Due to my research on landing positions I no longer believe that the dip phase must occur after a decision to swing. Also, I now define the start of any swing as the *aggressive commitment of the hips*. For identification purposes, let's refer to any hitter who uses the upright landing position as a "BIG DIPPER" and any hitter who rotates and tilts the torso early as a "LEAD-IN HITTER".

BAT POSITION OPTIONS

Do you know the hardest part of creating this new landing position? It is leveling out the bat. Do you know why? Because it is totally unnecessary. For similar reasons, it is equally as hard for me to write about it in this book. Let me ask you a question. If you're going to swing slightly up, why not hold the bat flattened out and lower right in your stance as seen in Figure 4-28?

I know. What about Ted? He held his bat vertically. Well, I stood in his kitchen a year and a half ago and I got into a stance with the bat

FIG 4-27 (a-b, left to right). *Photo sequence (a-b) shows how a well balanced landing should be able to withstand a firm push backward or forward.*

FIG 4-28. *After years of studying the details of hitting, if I had to choose one batting position which I thought was best it would be the one shown here.*

flattened out and the hands low. Knowing damn well that I could make a great case in defense of this seemingly odd stance and knowing that Ted himself stood with his bat differently, I lured my teacher into a sparring session. I said, *"Ted, why not just start with the bat right here?"* But, there was no sparring session. Instead, being the number one forefather of technical hitting, he bellowed, "Why not!" Then he started naming guys left and right who were successful hitters from stances with low flattened bat positions...

Why did Ted hold his bat vertically? Well, for one reason he personally liked the lighter weight when the bat is held perpendicular to the ground. But hitters don't hit from their stance. They hit from their landing! Therefore, having to bring the bat down to the flattened position from a higher position in the stance is an unnecessary movement. I'd much rather hold the weight of the flattened bat right in my stance. Hitting is a sequence of movements. I feel that the stance, like any other phase of hitting, has a responsibility to serve the needs of the movements to follow.

Why have the bat head any further away from the average contact point than it has to be? After all, the greater the distance the full swing must travel, the more movements required, and thus the harder it is. If this were darts, flattening the bat from another position would be the equivalent of starting the dart at your waist, bringing it up to your nose, and shooting it all in one motion. It doesn't make sense. My prediction is that more bats will flatten out in the future.

I think the main reason Ted held his bat vertically was to look good. The stories of Ted wanting to be a good looking hitter are plentiful and as a skinny kid in front of thousands of people I

think he liked the strong and acceptable look of the vertical bat. Who doesn't want to look good in sports?

In summary a hitter can land in two acceptable ways: 1) as a LEAD-IN HITTER or 2) as a BIG DIPPER. Before either of these landings the hitter basically has three options with the bat: A) the flattened bat with lower hands in the stance, B) flattening the bat during the stride (along with a lowering of hands if necessary), and/or C) looping it all under and up during the swing — with hip rotation. Combining the landing choice numbers with the bat option letters, let me show you how I rank them on a scale of technical quality first to last: 1A, 1B, 2A, 2B and 2C.

Through film and photos I have seen Ted use 2C and 1B. The most widely attempted combination today is 2C — by a landslide. But it is not executed well. While this marks progress to me, your question surely remains...Which one do you utilize?

As for the landing position, you'll have to sort it out for yourself. I can't say which one is better for you at this point in your career because I don't know you...your intelligence... your attitude. But don't let your age get in the way. If you think you can handle the "lead-in landing", go to it. It only gets harder as you get older.

As for the bat position I think we can get something done right now. Sad as it is, if you choose 1A or 2A with the bat flat and the hands low in your stance as seen in Figure 4-28, almost immediately you'll be instructed by everyone and their mother to bring the bat and your hands up. You'll be weird... If one of these people happens to make out the line-up, you may be forced to flatten the bat from another position. How do we get it down?

FIG 4-29 (a-b, left to right). *Dropping the bat down in the process of the cocking motion is the best place to drop if you chose not to flatten the bat postion in your stance.*

I do not like flattening the bat with the stride. I think it's tough to do and will likely endanger the quality of the stretch position and therefore reaching your potential. I think a good compromise is to flatten the bat at the start of the cocking motion as seen in Figure 4-29 (a-b).

Here the hitter can model a fashionable bat position in his stance and drop it down with the cocking of the hips. This will eliminate the dollar-seat critics and bring the bat to a good working position. Note that the cocking motion is the only phase of hitting that shares the overall feeling of back and down. If the bat has to go down after you start moving I think it belongs with its cousins in the cocking motion.

Similar to Ted, the hitter will also tap into the benefit of not having to hold the weight of the flattened bat in the stance. This is the best disguise I can provide. Good luck...

By the way, if we make this batting option "D", my technical rating order would now look something like this: 1A, 1D, 1B, 2A, 2D, 2B and 2C.

THE GLIDE

Regardless of whether you're a big dipper or a lead-in hitter, after the hitter lands, there is a short gliding motion that is very important. This gliding motion is executed by a slight rotation of the back knee which is initiated by a gas pedal-type push from the ball of the back foot. The front leg contributes by loading more weight and allowing the glide with a slight absorbing bend.

While gliding slightly forward the hitter has also started a controlled rotation. That is to say, the hitter is locked in the stretch position as his hips slowly tow the entire swing in a slight rotation as the body glides forward. This glide and tow should not be confused with the start of the swing. It is all very controlled and before any decision to aggressively drive the hips as shown in Figure 4-30 (a-c).

FIG 4-30 (a-c, left to right). *After the landing and while still stretched, the hitter will glide slightly forward and open just a bit. This sequence involves very little actual movement.*

FIG 4-31. *Here the hitter has lost the stretch in the glide leaving him out of position with a weak and worthless swing.*

Now gliding can be tricky. What's tricky is gliding and towing while maintaining the stretch. Many times, during the glide, young hitters will bring their shoulder line equal to their hip line or beyond. The minute this happens that specific swing is ruined, because the towing sequence of that one swing is broken. The hitter has allowed slack to come back in the swing. (The box car is catching up to the engine.) This is shown in Figure 4-31.

Another caution is overloading the front knee. If the hitter glides too far forward he will overload the front leg as a power source. This is then just controlled lunging and of little value. If the hitter brings too much weight over the front leg, his hip rotation will be sluggish, with his body and eyes popping up two to four inches during the swing. The longer the glide the less

FIG 4-32. *Here the front knee appears over the ball of the front foot meaning the hitter is at the extent of his glide.*

impressive the hip rotation. The glide must be very short. When your front knee starts to flow over the ball of your front foot that's about the maximum extent of the glide. This is shown in Figure 4-32.

THE MOVEMENTS OF THE ARMS

I don't believe there is anything more aggravating than to watch a hitter execute perfectly and then blow it all completely out the window with the arms, wrists, or hands. Unfortunately, it happens all the time and at all levels. And as you will see, even if a hitter is moving good before and during the swing, improper use of the arms, wrists, or hands will bury him. Yes, it's true that the pre-swing will prepare the hitter for ultimate bat speed and power; and yes, good hip rotation will then create it. But a hitter has got to realize that only the proper use of his arms, wrists, and hands can then apply what he's created. Remember, these body parts control the bat!

When speaking about arms, I find it best to trace their movements throughout the entire swing. This is due to the fact that most hitters today are big dippers with their bats and hands high — the longest of acceptable options (combination 2C, see landing and bat position options). I'm going to run the movements of arms throughout the swing, from an upright landing and an upright bat position. I will not start to flatten the bat until aggressive hip rotation starts the dip phase and the swing. By showing you the difficult responsibilities of using the arms correctly throughout the longest combination of landings and bat positions, I'm hoping that other options will not only become more significant but more attractive.

FIG 4-33 (a-c, left to right). *The angle of the front arm must remain locked in place throughout the stance, the cocking motion and the stretch position. This is illustrated in photo sequence (a-c).*

Beginning with the stance in Figure 4-33a, we again see both arms bent, with my front arm slightly tense and my back arm — my power arm — relaxed. The next frame Figure 4-33b displays the cocking motion. Here again we see how the arms do not move on their own, but merely rotate back with the upper body as one unit and in the same position. As we go on to the stretch position Figure 4-33c, the arms pull back slightly; however, the movement is in the front shoulder joint, while the elbow joint of the front arm does not change its angle, and that's important.

Up to this point I have found the arm movements to be fairly easy to both learn and teach. However, after the hitter decides to swing, we find the movements to be much more difficult. Again, from an upright position of torso and bat, a decision to swing ignites the hips and the hitter starts to pull the entire swing down into the dip phase. It is a powerful looping of under and up, where the front elbow, as a weak link in the hitter's chain, is tested hard to properly connect the front side of the body to the back. The front elbow fights to remain tense and bent as the back elbow tucks in close and rides with the backside. The dipping of the back shoulder coupled with the rotation of the hips will direct the front elbow up and out of the way, while the back arm remains tucked and close to the body. These movements can be seen in Figures 4-34 (a-c).

FIG 4-34 (a-c, left to right). *When the hips enter into the picture, the front arm will be tested – it must not straighten out at this point of the swing. From this point, it will lead the swing by traveling up and out of the way.*

FIG 4-35 (a-b, left to right). *The hips having led the way, both arms now extend in unison – the bottom arm "pulling" while the top arm "pushes." Note that 4-35b is the moment just after contact.*

Now, the hips having led the way, both bent arms will extend, with the bottom arm pulling as the top arm pushes. Again, these movements should take place in unison. This can be seen in Figure 4-35 (a-b). Note that in Figure 4-36 (a-b) I have crushed a piece of cardboard with the same movements.

FIG 4-36 (a-b, left to right). *Using a piece of cardboard, the movements of the top and bottom arm are again displayed. Notice how the elbows bend the cardboard.*

Why do I want tension in the front arm? The answer lies in the fact that when a hitter starts his hip rotation, the circular momentum that's created places an overwhelming jerk on the front arm, causing a natural tendency for it to then drift back — straighten out. It is here where the movement difficulty begins. The front arm must combat this strain and prevent itself from straightening out too early. I call this anchoring the front arm, and it's done best by preparing the arm for this sudden strain with a slight bit of tension right in the stance. With this tension, the bent front arm will now first pull the bat and power arm around with the rotation of the upper body guarding and preserving the position of the bat and arms in relation to the upper body. This allows both arms to remain bent while they await a double arm extension into the potential contact area. Both arm movements can be seen in Figures 4-37 (a-d) and 4-38 (a-d).

FIG 4-37 (a-d, top to bottom). *Photo sequence (a-d) traces the top arm through the key points of the swing.*

FIG 4-38 (a-d, top to bottom). *Photo sequence (a-d) traces the bottom arm through the key points of the swing.*

Why all the caution? If the front arm pre-extends, whether it be in the stance, cocking motion, stretch position, or beginning of the swing, (the latter being the most common) the hitter will run into problems by changing the length of the lever in which he is swinging. With the front arm extended, the hitter now swings a lever that ranges in length from the end of the bat to his front shoulder; the shoulder being the pivot point. Figure 4-39 (a-b) displays the common problem of drifting the front arm at the beginning of the swing. Notice how the front arm has extended and now how it begins to drag the power, or top arm, out and away from the body as well. The drawbacks are endless.

First off, the hitter is now using a longer, heavier lever; that being, of course, the arm and bat as opposed to just the bat. Naturally, the hitter is slower and therefore loses time by having to commit himself (decide to swing) earlier. Also, the hitter is moving that lever (at least in the front arm) with a different group of muscles — the shoulder muscles — and it's

FIG 4-39 (a-b, left to right). *The hitter pictured in the above sequence displays the common tendency of a hitter to pre-extend his front arm at the beginning of the swing.*

much more difficult. How fast can you move an outstretched arm and bat from Point A to Point B as seen in Figure 4-40 (a-b)? Not very fast — it's much too heavy! Proper execution relies upon the upper arm muscles, not the shoulders. We want to use those muscles that control and support extension from the elbow joint.

FIG 4-40 (a-b, left to right). *When the arms extend too early, the main pivot point of the action comes up to the shoulders when it should remain at the elbows. This lengthens and adds weight to the entire swing. The hitter above displays this effect.*

FIG 4-41 (a-c, left to right). *The good hitter starts his rotation with both arms bent then fires them "straight" into the contact area like the tail end of a whip.*

FIG 4-42 (a-c, left to right). *The pre-extended hitter's bat travels in a "circular" path. This longer, heavier hitting tool now approaches the contact area from the side.*

The problems continue. If the arms do extend early, they will cause the hands and bat to travel in a circular path, and while a hitter's body certainly rotates, the bat and arms merely ride with it until it comes time to apply the momentum your body has created. At that time the arms fire the bat straight to the ball. This can be seen best in Figure 4-41 (a-c), where the dark line represents a high inside pitch.

In Figure 4-42 (a-c) we see improper arm movement caused by pre-extension. Notice how the pre-extended arms bring the hands and bat into contact in a circular path, where Figure 4-41 (a-c) displays the arms pushing into contact in basically a straight line. Naturally, the shortest distance between two points is a straight line and therefore the curved path of Figure 4-42 (a-c) has cost the hitter valuable time.

The pre-extended hitter is geometrically slower Figure 4-43.

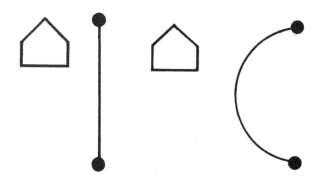

FIG 4-43. *This diagram shows a geometric comparison of correct and incorrect arm movement. In this simple example we can observe the lengthened path of the pre-extended hitter's hands and bat. It will take this hitter a longer period of time to reach contact.*

63

While I've got pre-extension with its back to the wall, let's look at its effect on the potential contact area (the area in which it is possible for the bat to hit the ball). When a bat approaches the path of the ball with a circular attack, it approaches more from the side, cutting down the possibility of contact by literally cutting down the amount of time the bat is actually in the potential contact area. In Figure 4-44 (a-d) correct arm movement keeps the bat in the potential contact zone much longer. In Figure 4-45 (a-d), the dark line again repre-

sents the path of an inside high pitch. Notice how long the fat part of the bat remains outside of the potential contact area due to pre-extended arms. The conclusion is that the pre-extended swing not only cuts contact percentage, but also requires better timing on the hitter's part.

It's not over yet! The pre-extended swing also causes the ball to be hit much further to the left for a right-handed batter or to the right for a left-hander which often is well foul from an even stance (I'll elaborate). This can be seen in Figure 4-46 (a-b).

FIG 4-44 (a-d, left to right). *The good hitter keeps the preferred area of the bat in the contact area as much as possible and therefore maximizes contact potential.*

FIG 4-45 (a-d, left to right). *The pre-extended hitter will not have the preferred area of the bat in the contact area anywhere near as long as the hitter with good technique. Contact potential for the pre-extended hitter is significantly reduced.*

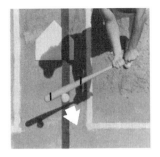 

FIG 4-46 (a-b, left to right). *Here we see the approach angle of a bat launched from a hitter with proper arm execution in 4-46a, and pre-extended arm execution in 4-46b. Notice the angle in which the ball will be hit along with the contact area.*

Though I'll talk about this in more detail later, where the ball is hit on the field is an element of your style and extremely important. This problem of hitting balls more to the left or right stems from the angle in which the hitting surface of the bat comes into the contact area. A step further, in Figure 4-47 (a-b), we see not only the approaching angle of the bat but also the available batting surface provided at contact by correct and incorrect technique. This concept may be easier to understand where I have displayed the same basic arm approach with a tennis racket. As you can see, correct arm execution will also provide a greater batting surface along with balls hit in their proper direction.

Another hassle is that pre-extended arms create a weaker hitting lever. Remember, in the pre-extended swing, the hitting lever is from the shoulder to the end of the bat. This lever has

FIG 4-47 (a-b, top to bottom). *Using a tennis racket to amplify the point of available contact area, compare the batting surfaces of the two approaches pictured above.*

two major weaknesses; the elbow joint and the wrists. Due to the length of the lever, both the elbow joint and wrists will give quite a bit at contact, costing the hitter a valuable loss of power. While it is true that the wrists and elbow joints also give with proper arm movement, the arms are behind the contact — behind the lever as opposed to beside it, and therefore the give is much less. These weaknesses can be seen in Figure 4-48.

FIG 4-48. *Contact made behind the bat is much stronger than contact made beside it.*

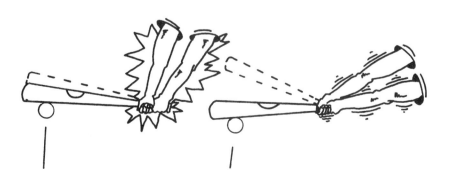

FIG 4-49. *Good arm execution brings the bat to contact maximizing the strength of the wood or aluminum bat material. Poor arm execution allows for the weaknesses of three joints and a grip.*

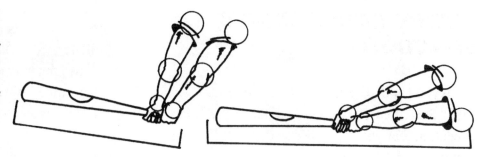

Also, with proper arm movement, the attacking lever is only the length of the bat and therefore composed of a consistent substance being wood or aluminum as opposed to wood or aluminum plus bones and flesh. The pre-extended hitter must be much stronger to both swing and support this faulty lever.

I'll tell you another thing: balls hit toward the end or handle of a bat supported correctly are hit much harder, therefore the hitter with proper technique has more room for error. He'll end up with more blood hits. Levers are compared in Figure 4-49.

Certainly, the pre-extended swing's lever weight makes the pre-extended lever more difficult to control and therefore less consistent when trying to hit such a small target. From the angle of Figure 4-50a, we can picture the pre-extended hitter's tendency toward vertical fluctuations, while the same hitter swinging correctly swings a lighter and more controllable lever due to the technique of Figure 4-50b.

Though not as noticeable, the heavier lever is also harder for the entire body to swing. The hips and upper body will not rotate as quickly if the arms drift away from the body at any time.

My conclusion is that the pre-extended hitter must be stronger, quicker, have better timing, and the ability to make rushed decisions. The hitter that finds success with pre-extension is miles from his potential.

I'm sure you can see why I'm so concerned with using the arms correctly, but I think my case becomes even more dramatic when one understands that, mechanically speaking, pre-extension is possibly the most common and destructive problem in hitting. Very rarely do I observe good arm execution at any level, and it hurts to watch it needlessly wither away at good contact percentage, and therefore baseball action and interest. However, when a former major league batting instructor demonstrates excessive pre-extension as proper technique (pages 122-130 of Lau's book), it's not hard to understand why.

FIG 4-50 (a-b, left to right). *The hitter who turns the corner with the arms and hands tight will be more consistent at hitting his targets. He will also make much stronger contact on mistakes (when the top or bottom half of the ball has struck as opposed to the center).*

PLATE COVERAGE AND BAT SELECTION

If you're on the ball you may be saying to yourself, "Sure, that was a great explanation of arm execution, but you can't reach the outside corner that way and, therefore, it's useless." Well, I don't think it's useless, but most times you're right about the outside corner. With good execution, 26-inch arms, and while standing 13 inches away from the plate in an even stance, I need a 36-inch bat to deal with the outside corner. Now, I'm a fairly big guy at 6'2", and what I'm getting at is that smaller guys with shorter arms are even less capable on the outside portion of the plate. Through the eyes of good mechanical arm execution, the bats most hitters use today are much shorter than they should be.

Naturally, whenever I say longer, which many times means heavier as well, everybody starts screaming bloody murder. But when we make an example of Ted himself, standing 12 to 13 inches off the plate using a 35-inch bat with about 27-inch arms (armpit to palm), what I'm saying starts to sound logical. In relation to Ted's arm length and the distance he stood from the plate, a 35-inch bat was necessary if he was going to use his arms correctly and still be able to cover the width of the strike zone.

If Ted had used a 33-inch bat he would have had to sacrifice one of two things: either bat speed and power due to the use of pre-extension for plate coverage, or plate coverage on the outside corner due to the shorter bat. The point — the smaller-armed hitter is getting railroaded. He's swinging a shorter, lighter bat with pre-extended arms. Also, he's losing bat speed, power and consistency when he could be quicker, stronger, and more consistent by swinging a longer and heavier bat correctly.

I know what you're thinking... the smaller guys with the smaller arms aren't strong enough to handle the longer, heavier bats. You're wrong. The shorter-armed hitter isn't physically weak. He's much stronger than he's given credit for, but he hasn't had the platform to prove it. He has been forced to pre-extend by circumstances beyond his control, and as a result he has become mechanically weak (will elaborate). Certainly, you can understand that how you use your body — its angles and their movements — will have a direct effect on your efficiency. Well, this is the problem with the shorter-armed hitter. He is less than what he could be before and during contact. He is slower and weaker by using his arms incorrectly and by stepping up to the plate with the wrong bat.

When people wonder why some of these smaller stocky guys don't hit more home runs, many times they need not look any further than the bat in the hitter's hands and the way it's being brought into and supported at contact. Think about it. Do you think Ted Williams possessed any more of a natural ability to hit home runs than Pete Rose? No way! What makes a powerful hitter? It's momentum (a weight times a velocity). And when momentum is applied correctly, the more you generate, the harder the ball will be hit. Though Williams was taller than Rose, I don't believe Ted had the ability to generate as much momentum as Pete. Lau's book lists Rose at 192 pounds in 1979, which is very close to Ted's mature playing weight of 190 pounds. However, Pete has been a much faster runner than Ted, which breaks down to mean that Pete has had the leg ability to move his 192 pounds much faster than Ted's 190 pounds. I think you can see where I'm going. What dictates the speed of the swing? Hip rotation. And what controls hip rotation? Legs.

AP/Wide World Photos

AP/Wide World Photos

FIG 4-51 & 4-52 (left to right). *Side by side the bodies and swings of hitters Ted Williams and Pete Rose bring to life the importance of approach for hitters and coaches.*

A step further, if we had them both in their prime, who would you bet on to bench press (an exercise that requires similar movements and muscles use as good arm execution) the most amount of weight? Sorry, Ted. Rose has clearly possessed long-ball ability. Why wasn't he more productive in the power categories? The answer lies in plate coverage, bat selection and pre-extension! Rose's power, like so many other hitters, was lost from the shoulders down. Mechanically speaking, Williams made up for and surpassed Rose's natural speed and untapped power by using the bat that would allow him to use his arms correctly, and therefore apply his momentum more efficiently.

To get a better idea of what I mean, look at these photos of Pete and Ted. For a hundred bucks, who's the stronger of the two? That shouldn't take long to answer. Look at Rose's arms and legs in comparison to the Splendid Splinter. These pictures, side by side, say a thousand words. Look at the bat Pete has. I'd be willing to bet it's a 33-inch. Notice the location of Rose's arms — how far they are away from his body. His arm position is much like Figure 4-49.

Now, please don't get me wrong. This comparison is not an effort to down Pete Rose. He is truly a great. But I feel the comparison relays the important fact that the shorter-armed hitters have been, and continue to be, forced toward the wrong bat, toward pre-extension, and therefore, toward an inferior hitting approach. How and why has this happened?

I'm going to save the main culprit for later because it requires separate attention, but for now, let's look at some others. The difficulty of anchoring the front arm, coupled with a decrease of instruction and practice, slowly drew the model hitters into a pre-extended swing. Once pre-extension became the norm, smaller and lighter bats had to come with it. That's because when you're pre-extended, smaller and lighter bats are the only bats you can swing.

Do you know what happens next? Well, the kids follow the pros and the bat manufacturers follow the buck. At a point, I think everybody was swinging 32's and 33's. So, of course the bat people are going to meet the popular demand. If you read this book in 1988 and ran out to find a 36-inch bat, you should have dressed like Indiana Jones because it would have taken that to find one. Bats aren't much bigger today, but I see more 35's and hitters at every level are reaching for a slightly longer bat. You know — a 32 rather than a 31 or a 34 as opposed to a 33. That's a sure sign that they are swinging a little better and they are.

I think it is interesting to see the evolution of this specific problem and how the pieces come together. Television cuts out the minor leagues. The loss of the minor leagues cuts practice. The cut of practice draws the arms away from the body. The fan pays to see the pre-extended hitter. The television showcases him. The innocent kid copies him. All the pre-extended hitters need shorter bats. After a couple of years the bat manufacturers are stuck with big bats and so they stop making them. If the professional changes his mind, he can get any bat he wants. But what does the kid do?

It's funny — the hitters of yesterday used longer, heavier bats. Why? Man was smaller, had shorter arms and less strength. Why would hit-ters ever want to reach for a larger bat? According to Hillerich & Bradsby, there were many bat orders over 36 inches. And remember, this was when baseball was booming and highly competitive — truly the national pastime. Where is the logic? The way I see it, hitting was indeed much better; and on the average, these smarter hitters knew how to use their arms and understood not only that they needed a certain bat to execute to potential, but also that good mechanics could swing that bat efficiently.

Sure, most people will think I'm crazy for saying that a guy like Rose would have been much better off with good arm execution, and a 35-ounce 37-inch bat (just a guess). But isn't it funny, the rules read that a bat can be up to 42 inches long. Is that a foolish rule? I wonder how many baseball authorities of today are smarter than the game's creator?

Assuming you can have any bat you want, how do you find the one that's best for you?

FIG 4-53. *The right bat for each individual hitter will take some time to find. It should feel comfortable in your hands to begin with. Then, be certain it is sized so that you can cover all areas of the strike zone and still handle the average fastball in your league.*

When first selecting a bat I recommend, as Ted did, that you choose something that feels good in your hands — something you think you can handle. However, this can be confusing because real good bat selection can only occur after the hitter adopts a sound mechanical approach. How can you pick a bat before you experience your length need, speed, or strength with good mechanics? I know my bat changed quite a bit with the development of my swing. And just as I have seen when teaching, the tendency was toward something longer and heavier.

After you can swing, the ideal bat for you is a bat that will enable you to cover the outside and low pitch with good arm execution and still be quick up and in. The best way to find it is to stand at the plate the way you would in a game and go through your swing in slow motion with the outside and low strike in mind. When you reach the assumed contact point, freeze and examine your mechanics (especially your arms). If they're good, you've got your length; and now you simply test its weight against the average high fastball that you'll face. There's an experimentation period here, and it's an important one. Take your time.

Going a bit further on the subject of bat length, if we were to picture all hitters standing in the exact same batter's box position, I feel the combination of bat and arm length from the outside corner of the plate into the front shoulder should add up to be about the same distance for all hitters. Listen, everybody's got to cover the same distance, whether it's with a longer bat or longer arm. This is seen in Figure 4-54. Unfortunately, today we have a relation that's more like the one seen in Figure 4-55. And it just doesn't add up.

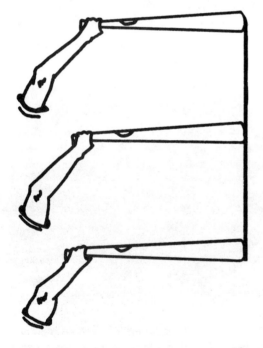

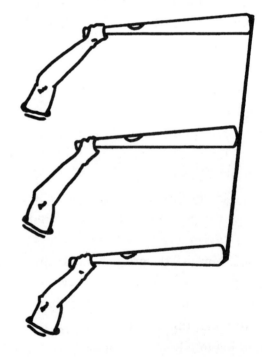

FIG 4-54. *Here we see an example illustrating how the longer-armed hitter should be holding the shorter bat while the shorter-armed hitter should be holding the longer bat. This makes perfect sense. All hitters must cover the strike zone regardless of their size.*

FIG 4-55. *Unfortunately for hitting today, the relationship between arm length and bat length generally looks like the example above. While the longer, weaker-armed hitters are swinging the longer bats, the stronger, shorter-armed hitters are swinging the shorter bats. Result? Pre-extension.*

FIG 4-56. *My good friend Bill Adams helps me convey the proper positioning of the arms, hands, and wrists at contact.*

THE WRISTS AND HANDS

Moving down to the wrists, we find them extending with the arms; not only creating additional momentum, but also controlling the angle in which the bat head makes contact with the baseball. Figure 4-57 (a-b) illustrates the bat head's movement caused by the wrists.

Also important is the position of the wrists

behind this approaching bat, which Ted called *unbroken wrists*. The bat must be supported correctly at contact. And as you can see in Figure 4-58, my wrists are behind the bat — behind the collision. Unfortunately, many times players will have their hands over the bat at contact, losing proper support and therefore complete application of force. This is what Ted called *rolling wrists*. It's a common problem and it will

FIG 4-57 (a-b, top to bottom). *As the arms extend into the contact point, the wrists will as well. The wrists have a hammering effect that is very strong at impact and the top hand is more dominant. Imagine hammering sideways into a wall – that should give you a feel for it.*

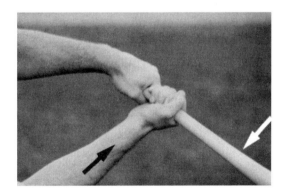

FIG 4-58. *At contact, the wrists are positioned "behind" the bat while the arms meet the plane of the pitch.*

hit your batting average like a wrecking crew. Take a look at Figure 4-59 (a-b). In these photos it's important to notice the position of both hands and how these positions could easily allow the bat to be pushed backward. Now the hands, the bat's key supporters, are in a weak position to support it in relation to the direction of the oncoming ball.

Also note in Figure 4-59a how the rolling wrist position will bring the hitter's bat to the top of the ball. As the top wrist rolls up and over the bat barrel will follow. Rolling wrists will distort your target area and feedback.

The name of the game is to have the least amount of give at contact. If some of the momentum goes toward pushing the bat backward, the projection force will be decreased and the hitter will lose a great deal of power. Hey, we want the bat to push the ball, not the ball pushing the bat. Ten times more important than possessing strong wrists and forearms is developing a contact point that is mechanically strong — fundamentally sound with unbroken wrists.

Learning how to make proper contact brings us to another subject of importance — grip. How

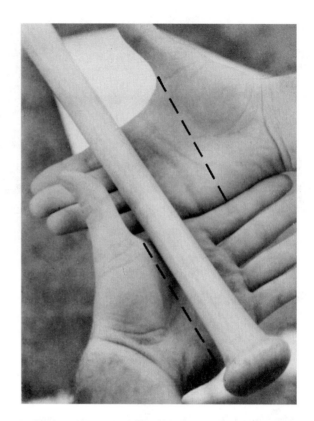

FIG 4-60. *Like Ted, I feel that the bottom hand should hold the bat like a hammer while the top hand holds it more in the fingers.*

you hold the bat in your stance will have a direct effect on how well your hands support it during contact. Like Ted, I feel the bottom hand holds the bat like you would a hammer, while the top hand holds it more toward the fingers. Figure 4-60 illustrates the bat's placement in each hand.

The top hand is held more in the fingers because when the ball is contacted correctly in the unbroken wrist position collision is extremely strong. When contacted on the fat part of the bat, this is not as obvious. However, if the hitter brings the bat into the collision just a hair late he will hit the ball more toward the handle of the bat. Here if the top hand is holding the bat deep in the palm, like the bottom hand, the handle of the bat will literally jam into the thumb joint and the hitter may be injured.

FIG 4-59 (a-b, left to right). *The above photos provide the example of what "not to do" with the wrists. Note that rolling wrists cause the bat to hop toward the top of the ball.*

If a hitter does not hold the bat right, he's usually in for an array of nagging thumb and wrist injuries throughout his career — not necessarily enough to keep him from playing but certainly an uncomfortable distraction.

The grip should also be firm. You don't hit a baseball with a limp grip. No matter how many fingers are moving in a guy's stance, if he's smart he'll hold on tight when he starts to swing. Now, Lau warns against what he called white knuckles, claiming that a tight grip can cause tension in the whole swing. Well, I believe a player can have tension problems in his swing, but I don't believe it stems from holding the bat too tight. Just because your grip is firm doesn't mean your upper arms must be tense. These body parts are controlled by two totally different muscle groups. Can you squeeze a rubber ball without flexing your biceps? Sure you can. If you know what you're doing and if you practice correctly, tension won't be a problem. I think people overdo the tension thing. Like statistics, tension is something everybody can talk about, and so they do. My thinking is similar to that of Lefty O'Doul — tension comes from fear, uncertainty, and a lack of confidence. If you're tense, it should therefore tell you that you've got some work to do.

Lau also feels that your grip should be firm, but relaxed with a personal knuckle alignment. I don't agree. How can your grip be firm and relaxed? That's like trying to sleep standing up. To me, firm is firm and relaxed is relaxed. If I have to apply any pressure, I'm not relaxed. You can only have one or the other; and when you're trying to turn around an 80-mile-an-hour fastball, it best be firm.

I don't like his theory on knuckle alignment either. If you're swinging slightly up, I feel there is a universal knuckle alignment. Counting from the fingertips, the second knuckle on the index finger of the top hand lines up between the second and third knuckles on the bottom hand. I believe this to be the best grip for covering all locations with good support at contact.

I'll tell you, though, if I knew a guy was going to keep it at my knees all day, I might consider moving my second knuckles closer together because that's a better position for a low ball. On the other hand, if a guy was up letter high all day, I may consider moving in the other direction; that is, top seconds toward bottom thirds. The problem is you don't know whether they're going to keep it down or up, and therefore you're better off playing the percentages with the grip I suggested. This alignment is seen in Figure 4-61.

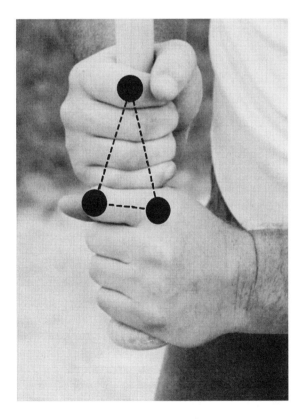

FIG 4-61. *To support solid contact through the slight up plane and against the average strike zone location, I feel that the knuckles should be aligned as shown above.*

FIG 4-62 (a-b, left to right). *The common and comfortable knuckle alignment pictured above will allow give and possible injury at contact.*

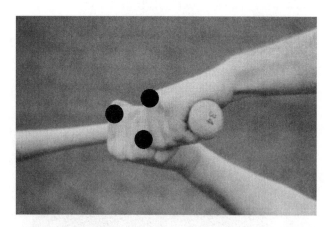

FIG 4-63. *The grip pictured here drives the top hand forearm directly behind the grip and on the same plane as the oncoming pitch.*

Now, in your stance, this knuckle alignment usually feels a bit uncomfortable; don't let that bother you. Remember, you don't contact the ball in your stance. This grip is comfortable at contact where it counts. If you settle for a comfortable grip in your stance, watch what can happen. Figure 4-62 (a-b) shows a common comfortable knuckle alignment and the problems it can lead to at contact. Notice how the wrists and therefore the arms are not really behind the bat at contact, leaving the bat less supported than it could be and therefore more vulnerable to give, whereas in Figure 4-63 we see a proper knuckle alignment leading to a position where the forearms are behind the bat, giving full support.

A hitter should note that after a week of this knuckle alignment, much like riding a new bicycle, the discomfort or newness will disappear. Don't associate comfortable with right.

Now, I've heard people argue that a hitter should squeeze on contact, and while it's true that you would be just a little quicker doing it that way, I don't advocate it because I don't believe the contact point is that easy to predict. If you're late squeezing, you may lose a hit due to frail support at contact, even though the swing was perfectly timed. Also, the tendency is to move your hands around the bat when you swing; that is to say the swing momentum changes your knuckle alignment. Another problem with it is that when you squeeze, the bat tends to move vertically. Hey, if it rises one-quarter of an inch, you could lose out.

The bottom arm wrist, much like the bottom arm, can also be thought about as a part of the swing that guides. The bottom wrist controls (from the pitcher's view) how the bat is positioned horizontally at contact. Naturally, to increase contact percentage we want the bat to be level. The bottom wrist will fluctuate the position of the bottom hand from up on the low ball to down on the high ball. These movements will keep the bat as level as possible throughout the different heights of the strike zone. Figure 4-64 (a-c) shows the position of the wrist for a level bat at three different strike zone heights.

Now, you may claim that I'm contradicting myself on the high pitch because the bottom wrist is not totally behind the bat and therefore not supporting the bat as well as it could. Well, though both the arms, wrists, and hands support the contact point, the top arm, wrist and hand — the ones closest to the contact point — supply most of the support to the collision of bat and ball. The way I see it, the bottom hand's first job is to let the top hand do its job correctly.

Although what we're really addressing is an arm caution, while we're talking about give and the support needed to prevent it, hitters should also be aware of the fact that the shoulder joints also can give and cause a weakening at contact. You know, it's funny — the skill of hitting is surrounded by talk that leads you to believe that it is one graceful, relaxed movement. But as you grow to understand it you'll find it quite the contrary. After a swing decision, hitting becomes a grunting skill, a skill of aggression — something fast and strong.

I never thought about hitting in this way until I learned the basics of a good swing. By changing my movements through *The Science of Hitting*, I found myself more aggressive and more confident. It is a lack of knowledge that describes the movements of this skill differently than what they are. Hitting isn't flower picking! Its got some guts to it. Or as Ted would say, "It's got some Oomph!"

HIGH PITCH

MID PITCH

LOW PITCH

FIG 4-64 (a-c, top to bottom). *The bottom wrist helps control the level of the bat from the hands to the bat head. The above photos denote different heights along with the corresponding position of the bottom wrist.*

THE HEAD AND EYES

Maybe I was brainwashed, but I didn't believe it. I didn't want to. And at first, you won't either. But you do not watch the ball hit the bat! I know you've heard it just as I have: *"Keep your eye on the ball,"* but it's not completely true. In a hitting discussion with Ted, he mentioned that the head and eyes go toward the anticipated direction of the hit, implying that the hitter does not watch the ball to contact. Naturally, I questioned him further, and his conclusion was that you don't watch the ball all the way in. I then questioned the stories of Ted's eyes, the greatest eyes in baseball; the eyes that could see what stitch was hit, that could read revolving record labels, and could see the ball actually hit the bat. *"That's all garbage,"* he answered. What Ted was claiming was that any hitter, himself included, sees the ball out in front of him (tunneling), and if he does swing his head should rotate with the rest of his body.

Though this sounds radical at first, it caught my attention because I always felt as though I was cutting my hip rotation short by keeping my head in. I also felt that when I dropped my eyes and head to try and see the ball better, ironically, I lost sight of the pitch. Looking back now, I realize that both my claims were true. Hey, your head is the top axis of your hip rotation. If you stick it down, you create a counter movement in your entire swing because everything else is rotating in the other direction. Hitters who drop their heads lose speed, power, and time by cutting down hip action and therefore slowing their swings down. As far as losing sight of the ball, I was on target there also. If a hitter drops his head, he loses sight of the ball, then faces a challenge to try and pick it up again and hit it square. This is a difficult task indeed.

The thing that really perked up my experimentation on this issue was a simple test that Ted used to convince me of his claim. He asked me to focus my sights on a sign about 60 feet away. After I did he then held his finger about four or five feet in front of me, a sure strike, a little lower than my letters. He said, "Okay. When I say 'now,' you look at my finger as quick as you can." When I did he confirmed, *"See, it took you just a split second to refocus, didn't it?"* When I agreed, the point became clear. How can anybody drop their head or eyes, causing them to lose sight, and then attempt to regain sight and focus on a moving object traveling 80 or 90 miles an hour, when they can't even do it with a stationary object? The answer is, it can't be done. It's impossible. Terry Bahill, a Carnegie-Mellon University Professor, declared *"Keeping your eye on the baseball is physiologically impossible."* Bahill, in a study done with students, amateur players, and major league players, found that not one subject, even ones with exceptional motor skills, could track a baseball closer than six feet at ninety miles per hour. "Humans simply cannot track targets moving with such high angular velocities." The best hitters, he then theorized, aren't those who can track the flight of the ball from the pitcher to the bat, but those who correctly guess where the ball will be at the moment of contact.

As far as I'm concerned, when the ball gets to a certain point, you've got a choice; you can keep your head in, and lose both sight of the ball and time, or you can rotate your head and eyes to where the ball should be hit, still losing sight of the ball but gaining time. I'll take the time. Using your head and entire body correctly with proper mechanics gives a hitter more time to see, therefore helping to keep good pitches merely good rather than making them great through the sluggish eyes of poor technique. Proper movement of the head is one more way of gaining time.

Chapter 5 of Lau's book is entitled "Your Head Goes Down When You Swing." And I read the Boston Globe one Sunday in 1982 and they had Walt Heriniak (former Red Sox batting coach), on how to hit a baseball. And one of his helpful points was, "Your head goes down when you swing." I remember distinctly it was right alongside, "You hit off your front foot."

Sure, on a low ball your head drops a little, but it drops while the ball is well out in front, and that's okay because you won't lose sight of it out there. When it comes time to hit that low pitch, however, your eyes and head will be on the way out. The head movement that makes me cringe and you less the hitter is demonstrated in Figure 4-65 (a-c).

Good movement of the head can be seen in Figure 4-66 (a-c). Notice at a certain point how the eyes have changed direction, along with the head tilted and looking toward the probable direction of the hit.

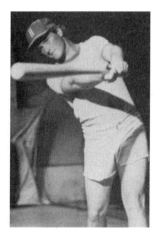

FIG 4-65 (a-c, left to right). *Photo sequence (a-c) demonstrates what I consider poor use of the head and eyes. Here, the head acts as a counter-movement to hip rotation while the eyes are expected to see what can't be seen.*

FIG 4-66 (a-c, left to right). *Photo sequence (a-c) shows the head and eyes, after doing their initial job, continuing to aid contact percentage by allowing the body to rotate freely, therefore maintaining speed and consistency.*

FIG 4-67. *The way that I check the efficiency of the head and eyes in relation to the swing is by standing on the pull side of the cage. From the view which you see in the above photo, I watch the hitter's head and eyes and listen for contact. On a high, inside pitch the hitter should be looking my way before I hear contact. In this example you will see how the hitter is looking left just before the ball hits the bat.*

Style Is Not Technique

What is a hitter's style? You hear about it all the time. But what exactly is it? Are the words style and technique interchangeable? Do they mean the same thing? Is a hitter's style how he hits? Or is it more subtle like the tightening of laces or the fit of a shirt or helmet? Baseball registers these words to mean the same, but they do not.

If I could correct only one flaw in hitting today, I would unquestionably choose to individually define the terms *style* and *technique*. The distinction between style and technique lies in the fact that style is personal and technique is universal. That is to say that style is an individual aspect of hitting, where technique should be basically the same for everyone. Of the two words, technique is not the word that's being misinterpreted. It is a method or an approach to a task. Style, however, is very different. Although an unavoidable aspect of hitting and a distinct feature of proper technique, style is not technique, but rather the direction in which the hitter must utilize his technique in order to reach potential.

I view style as an offensive position or an offensive role. Naturally, the correct role or style to play is simply the one that will be most productive in relation to your individual talent. Think about it, if Mo Vaughn and Nomar Garciaparra ran, fielded and threw with the same basic techniques, could they switch positions? Of course not. The reason prohibiting this would simply be an insufficient genetic makeup for the demands of the new style or role. Although Mo and Nomar may utilize the same bodily movements to run, field and throw, one player will undoubtedly be faster, taller, stronger, more aggressive, and so on. Therefore, individual capability eventually considers a player's potential in the realm of one role, position or style as opposed to another. Sad as it is, style is governed by talent!

FIG 5-1. *Digging in at the same plate where Mo Vaughn and Nomar Garciaparra take their swings, former student and Steve Ferroli Camp coach Hank Gibson goes to bat for Northeastern University in a college tournament game at Boston's Fenway Park.*

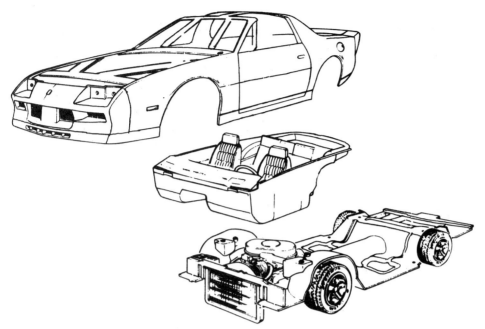

FIG 5-2. *Finding a hitter's basic style is much like putting a model car together – the available pieces can only go together to make a certain type of vehicle. An honest evaluation of talent will speed up the process of assembly.*

The confusion between the concept of style and technique has grown more complex due to the popular belief that style is something you create; in reality style is something you must realize. The direction, role, position or style that you will adopt as a hitter can only be found by giving a hard and honest look at your individual strengths and weaknesses. It's not such a difficult approach to understand. Think of like building a model car: you're not making the parts, you're simply piecing them together properly in a way that they look and fit best. The final product is the result of how well you assembled the parts based on what you had to work with.

If you dream up make-believe parts and continue to build upon them, sooner or later you'll face the sad realization that something is drastically out of place. Then with the glue long dry, the possibility of reaching the top shelf will be gone. Honesty is the key here.

"Hit according to your style," Williams warned. However, like so many other statements in hitting, this statement has been misinterpreted. People have twisted the message and continue to twist it to mean hit the way you want; that is, invent your own technique and then call that your style. I see and hear this all the time and it's placing the complex execution of how to hit a baseball on the shoulders of the young athlete; naturally, he can't handle it. Consequently, we're faced with thousands of personal, sub-par hitting techniques justified as style.

With a basic understanding of style, it's very important to zero in on your style and the realization of it. Style is a complex part of hitting and reaching potential demands that every hitter find and utilize his own style correctly. To simplify this let's break style into two parts: *basic style* and *individual style*.

BASIC STYLE

While it is true that each hitter holds his own style, it is also true that hitters and their styles (like shortstops and first baseman) can be placed into basic categories. Although, the categories or names you commonly hear — power hitter, singles hitter, opposite field hitter or "Punch-n-Judy" to name a few — convey inaccurate connotations, I strongly believe that similar but better defined categories would be extremely helpful to the understanding of style and the actualization of potential.

Therefore, I have identified and defined four different hitting categories which clearly reflect a hitter's intended role, position or direction at the plate. I call these *basic style categories*, or you may choose to think of them as a hitter's basic style.

A hitter's basic style is the groundwork or platform from which he will best launch his technique. Consequently, discovering basic style should be approached with care. Here the

FIG 5-3. *When I think of basic style and technique, I think of cars. There are sports cars, station wagons, mid-sized coupes and punch buggies. But they all run on fuel. They all need oil, water and a license plate. They are the same but different.*

hitter must honestly self-analyze and evaluate his major strengths and weaknesses. A few examples would include: attitude, intelligence, footspeed, quickness, power, coordination and courage. Then, after he has passed an honest judgment upon himself, he must match his capabilities with the demands of a compatible basic hitting style. From this point begins the long road of practice, working to perfect technique within the basic hitting style adopted as one's own.

The Pull Hitter

The most difficult hitting style is that of the *pull hitter*. A right-handed pull hitter usually hits the ball between the left field line and the second baseman position; a left-handed pull hitter can be expected to hit between the right field line and the shortstop position. A hitter with this style bats in an even stance, making the general contact area much closer to the pitcher than the other styles that will be discussed. Unfortunately, this factor cuts down both reaction time and margin of contact error. As a result, the pull hitter must be quick with the bat.

The pull hitter should also be a long ball threat. Before getting in the position of a two-strike count, he must be capable of consistently creating enough momentum to potentially knock any speed of pitch into the seats (that is, any pitch which should be pulled). The pull hitter must be extremely smart, selective, patient and observant, as he will be pitched to very carefully and therefore must prepare for and read pitches very well.

Before two strikes the pull hitter must get the ball in the air. His target area mistakes should be on the "up side" of up or down, therefore rendering fly balls and pop-ups.

The Middle Man

The *middle man* is the most common hitting style. This right- or left-handed batter hits balls from the shortstop/third-base hole to the second-base/first-base hole. The middle man bats from a slightly closed stance, creating a contact area farther from the pitcher than the pull hitter, therefore establishing more reaction time. The middle man is not consistently a long ball threat though he may get his share of home runs and extra base hits. It is a plus if he's a relatively fast runner, as his contact area will cause many balls to be hit up the middle and to the outfield gaps. However, this is not imperative.

Unlike the power hitting styles, the middle man will most often be made to hit. Therefore he must guard against being overaggressive at the plate. Before two strikes, the middle man's target area of mistakes should range from hard ground balls to fly balls — no pop-ups or weak ground balls.

The Power Middle Man

The *power middle man* is the most physically powerful hitter of the four basic hitting styles. He bats from a slightly closed stance and hits the ball from the shortstop/third-base hole to the second-base/first-base hole. His contact points are set further away from the pitcher than the pull hitter's giving him more time to read the incoming pitch. Although this hitter is not as quick as the pull hitter, he should be every bit as smart since he also will be pitched to very carefully.

Before two strikes, the power middle man has the ability to consistently create enough momentum to hit the ball over the center field fence on any speed pitch. This hitter is usually a slow runner. Before two strikes he also tries to get the ball in the air. His target area mistakes, like the pull hitter, should be on the *up side* of up or down, again rendering fly balls or pop-ups.

The Singles Hitter

The *singles hitter* is extremely fast. He has the ability to beat out any difficult infield play and steal second base almost at will. His strength is in making contact. For contact assurance this hitter uses a shortened swing (will elaborate). He also hits up the middle as described for the two middle men. The singles hitter must also be very patient because he will be made to hit. Due to his speed he will rarely walk. Again, a .300 hitter fails seven out of ten times. And because singles hitters are not long ball threats, the tendency is to go right at them, which can lead to overaggressiveness and poor pitch selection.

Before and during two strikes, the singles hitter's target area mistakes should be on the "*down side*" of up or down. His mistakes will render hard and weak ground balls but generally not produce fly balls or pop-ups. The singles hitter is the best two-strike hitter of the four basic styles. However, he should not be in the position to bat with two strikes that often and certainly he should find himself there less often than players having the other three styles.

If you understand the significance of each basic style category and have the ability to honestly self-evaluate your individual talent areas, then you will probably be able to find the basic style that fits you best. When you do, you must then take it on to the field to confirm your choice. Take your time. The general hitting areas for each style can be seen in Figures 5-4 and 5-5.

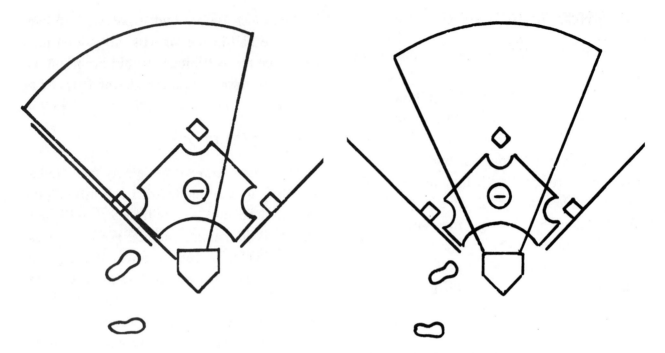

FIG 5-4. *This diagram shows the area in which the "pull hitter" hits. For a right-handed batter it ranges from the left field line to the second baseman (for a left-handed batter it ranges from the right field line to the shortstop position).*

FIG 5-5. *This diagram shows the area in which the "power middle man", "middle man", and "singles hitter" hit. It applies to both right- and left-handed hitters and ranges from the shortstop/third-base hole to the second-base/first-base hole.*

INDIVIDUAL STYLE

What about the refined part of style — *individual style*? After a hitter begins to utilize good technique after settling into a suitable basic style, he is then ready to start finding and developing his individual style. When I think of individual style, I think of it as the last staircase leading to a hitter's potential. I mean, once he's got the basics down and is directing his main strengths and weaknesses through his basic style, the next step is logically a fine tuning process — a focus on the hitter's subtle strengths and weaknesses. Individual style asks the question, "What personal adjustments must I make to bring my ability and technique to potential?

Now subtle may not be the best word to describe some of the adjustments I'm referring to because they are very important. Mechanically speaking, individual style covers issues like: distance from the plate, bat selection, location of both the rip and middle areas, pitch selection (type of pitch), rhythm and offsetting weight. Mentally speaking, it looks to the following: all phases of spring preparation, attitude, practice routine and dealing with pressure. Individual style also runs into the psychological part of the hitter; analyzing quirks, superstitions and fears. Individual style is a small part of hitting approach in which the hitter makes personal approach decisions.

Physically, mentally and psychologically... these things add up.

THE STRIDE (PURPOSE AND STARTING TIME)

The purpose of the following sections is to convey why, when, how and where you should stride. Though the stride's association with the stretch position alone confirms its mechanical prominence, its entanglement with style, timing, and the overall quality of the swing demands a more detailed explanation. Due to the stride's central position in the chain of hitting mechanics, a strong understanding of the following material should not only enrich your present approach, but also help with the ongoing chore of correction and adjustment.

There is no way you can understand stride's importance or its execution until you first understand its purpose. Why do hitters stride? Basically, hitters stride for one reason, and that is to gain preliminary body momentum before and during the hitter's decision to swing. The hitter uses his stride like a headstart. That is to say, he uses it to get his body moving before he actually knows what or where the pitch is, and therefore whether he wishes to swing or not. By moving the body (breaking inertia) before his decision, the hitter will not have to waste time getting his body moving after a decision to swing. Therefore, when timed properly, this preliminary body momentum (or headstart) provides the hitter with more time.

Getting the body moving early is a great advantage. Think about it. If you were jogging and then suddenly decided to burst into a sprint, that first sprinting step would be much easier than from a dead stop because you were already moving. I mean, you didn't have to start the movement, you merely increased it. Stride does the same thing for the hitter — it primes and therefore enhances your swing.

With our purpose in mind, the starting time of the stride becomes critical. Though I said earlier that the ideal starting time was when the pitcher's arm came over his throwing shoulder, it's really the lower arm that marks the starting point. The hitter should start to stride before the high-speed extension of the pitcher's forearm and wrist toward the plate. The hitter is clearly starting his stride before the ball has been released, and that must be understood. If the hitter starts striding after the release point, or even during the release point, he is late — he's behind the ball because he's behind with his movements and, as a result, his headstart advantage is then forfeited. The ideal starting time can be seen in Figures 5-6 and 5-7.

FIG 5-6 & 5-7 (top to bottom). *Here, my brother Rick helps to convey the starting point of both the cocking motion and the stride (stretch position).*

I have found hitters at all levels to be late striding and foolishly handing away a good portion of their potential success. Many times hitters with both fine swings and attitudes will go through their careers being less than what they could have been simply because they didn't know how to stride on time. It's sad. It's like practicing a piano solo and then starting it a measure late every concert. All the hard work you've done on your solo (your swing) is depressingly soured because the solo can only be dynamic if it comes in at the correct time.

Certainly, the good hitters don't miss their cue. As much as I've disagreed with Lau's work, he conducted a great film study on the 1980 all-star game that showed every hitter starting his stride before the ball had been released. No one was dead late striding the entire game. Why then is late striding such a problem?

LATE STRIDING

The cause of late striding is fear, not so much the fear of being hit but more of swinging too early. Swinging early holds a place of horror in every hitter's mind. The early swing usually succeeds in making a spectacle of the hitter in a broken-down half-hearted display. It is the highest plateau of mechanical embarrassment for hitting and therefore feared the most. Though the stride movements themselves are fairly simple, a hitter trying to learn them on his own without any feedback or reinforcement may never overcome that fear of moving early and therefore never learn stride timing correctly. Naturally, the younger the hitter, the greater the fear.

This stems from the overall misconception that you must see the ball and then hit it. Sure, you've got to see the ball to hit it, but the con-notation has become to see the ball and then move, and that is *not* the way it's done. You do not have to see the ball before you move! I get irritated when I hear a coach use the popular saying, *"see the ball, hit the ball,"* because I know many kids will misunderstand and stride late. Better sayings would be *"move, see and hit"* or *"stride, see and hit"* because these sayings are a true reflection of the task.

On the other hand, as much as I hate this misconception, I can fully understand it. I mean, initially you would think that it's much smarter to see the ball before you start your stride, especially knowing that the pitcher can throw different pitches. Certainly, it sounds more logical than stepping out there without any information. But the fact of the matter is that it is impossible to hit in that fashion with consistency and authority. The ball is just traveling too fast in relation to moving your body in time.

Sure, you might get a piece by throwing your wrists and arms at the ball, but that's not hitting — that's just contact. *Hitting and contact are two different things.* Remember, hitting is a full body effort and if we expect the larger body parts to contribute by being positioned correctly at contact we've got to get them warmed up before we call on them to perform.

There is also a visual factor that has caused late striding. Regardless of the sport, it is often very difficult to notice a timing relationship between two body movements, like that found between the pitcher's arm and the start of the stride. Remember, these movements are taking place at the same time, 45 to 60 feet apart. Therefore, to see the relation between these movements, the observer must be behind either the pitcher or the hitter with both movements in view. Many times coaches are positioned poorly to teach stride timing. Hey, whether you're teaching a mechanic in hitting or someone to play the fiddle, if you can't see what's going on, how can you find faults, or correct them? You can't. And that's just what's happening. This simple mechanic is not understood or taught the way it should be.

STRIDE MOVEMENTS

At the very beginning of the stride, as the body starts to rock forward, we see two main movements: the entire body rocking forward and the parting movement of the upper and lower bodies to the stretch position. As previously discussed, both movements of the stretch position are initiated by muscle.

The rocking of the body forward (the forward swing of the pendulum), however, is not initiated by muscle, but is rather the result of the body's position in the cocking motion. If the front shoulder and knee have turned in and down and there is more weight on the back foot than on the front foot, the lifting of the stride leg will cause the body to come forward due to gravity. In Figure 5-8 the peak of the cocking motion reveals how the stride leg is holding back a pending forward force due mainly to the position of the shoulders. As you can predict, when the hitter lifts and begins to open his stride leg, he will automatically begin to fall toward his balance point.

Unfortunately, many times hitters will open their stride leg without rocking forward to balance. This should not be considered striding because if the hitter does not approach the balance point, he will have too much weight on the back foot and, as a result, less hip action when it comes time to swing. The stride is both the opening of the front leg and the forward rock or fall of the pendulum to balance. The hitter is opening his stride leg while his body falls toward the balance point.

Confusion often arises from the fact that so much happens during the flight of the stride. While the foot is in the air, the entire body will reach the stretch position and then, while in the stretch position, follow the path of the hips. Figure 5-9 runs through the relation between the upper and lower body during the flight of the stride.

FIG 5-8. *Due to the position of the shoulders, the peak of the cocking motion reveals how the stride leg is holding back a pending forward force. As you can predict when the hitter lifts and begins to open his stride leg, gravity will cause him to "fall" toward the balance point.*

Starting with Frame 1, we see the cocking motion with the upper body (shoulders) and lower body (hips) represented with lines. Progressing to Frame 2, we watch the beginning of the stride where the hips and shoulders begin to travel apart. Frame 3 shows the hitter in the stretch position at about mid-flight; and at this point the shoulders will not go back any further — they have stopped while the hips continue to pull forward. Frame 4 shows the hips overpowering and pulling the upper body with it. The upper body moves back only so long before the hips pull the entire body forward, establishing the hitter's headstart before the landing of the stride foot.

Though it's a very slight movement, you should note that a hitter's headstart is also in a circular pattern. I mean, if we're going to swing in a circular pattern, it only makes sense that our headstart should prime the same pattern, and it does. Towards the end of the stride's flight, after the body has reached the stretch position and the hips have started to turn the entire body with them, the body will start trying to turn the corner just slightly, and this turning movement

will continue through the landing of the stride into the glide. This is denoted by the large arrow in Frame 4.

Also, note that this circular start is a responsibility of the opening of the stride leg from the crotch. A stride leg that does not open but merely strides forward (a common problem) will do nothing for a circular headstart.

STRIDE DIRECTION

We can't forget direction. Where does the stride go? Toward the plate? Back at the pitcher? Parallel to the ball? Just where do you stride?

Before we talk about the main direction of the stride, it's important to first talk about direction solely in relation to the back foot. Regardless of the hitter's basic style and stance, the stride should land and mark the third point on an extended line that runs from the hitter's back heel through his front heel as seen in Figure 5-10 (a-b). Note that the even and closed stance both stride on this line I've described, even though their main direction differs.

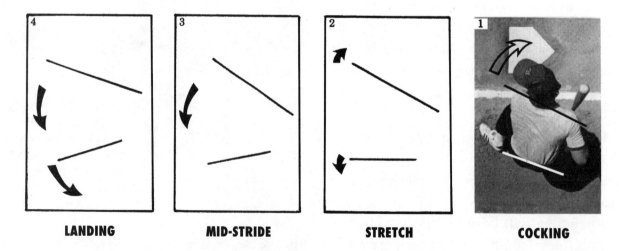

| LANDING | MID-STRIDE | STRETCH | COCKING |

FIG 5-9. *Cocking (Frame 1), Stretch (Frame 2), Mid-Stride (Frame 3), Landing (Frame 4). From the cocking motion of frame 1, the hitter strides forward in frame 2 while reaching the stretch position. By frame 3 the lower body has overpowered the hips and started to tow them in a circular motion. At the landing point in frame 4 this is still taking place but now becomes the responsibility of the glide.*

Why this heel line? Creating and striding along this line is merely another precaution taken to assure the hitter of proper hip rotation. If you rotate your feet from this line, they will line up beneath the hip that they are supporting, providing a well-balanced base and therefore enabling the hitter to tap his maximum range of circular motion and potential rotation momentum. This is seen in Figure 5-11 (a-c). On the contrary, if the heels do not line up, the hitter may find that his front leg is cutting his hip rotation short. Due to the base he has created with his stride, his back leg will actually start to bind against his front leg in the crotch area, slowing down his swing and inhibiting his range of motion. Figure 5-12 (a-c) displays the results of a poorly aligned base caused by a stride that has gone off the heel line.

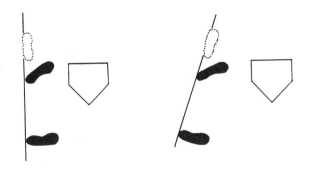

FIG 5-10 (a-b, left to right). *Regardless of style, the stride foot must land its heel on the heel line. Anytime a hitter breaks the heel line it will most often restrict hip rotation.*

FIG 5-11 (a-c, left to right). *The hitter who strides along the heel line assures good hip rotation and allows the feet to align with stability beneath the hip they are supporting.*

FIG 5-12 (a-c, left to right). *The hitter who crosses the heel line not only cuts hip rotation short, but also causes instability by creating a narrow, unbalanced base.*

Also important, in Figure 5-13 (a-b) you can see that these two different hitters have their back feet forming a right angle to their heel line. Though I said earlier (when talking about stance) that the back foot lies straight across, it's really perpendicular (at 90 degrees) to the heel line. The front foot's opened position (at about 45 degrees) is also only open in relation to the heel line. Due to the open front foot, if the feet are positioned correctly in the stance, the front toe will be slightly behind the back toe when compared to a line drawn parallel to the heel line. This is seen in Figure 5-14 (a-b).

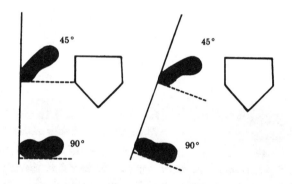

FIG 5-13 (a-b, left to right). *The front foot should be at approximately a forty-five degree angle to the heel line with the back foot resting at ninety degrees. This is shown above with both the pull hitter and middleman heel line.*

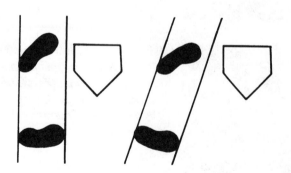

FIG 5-14 (a-b, left to right). *The forty-five degree angle of the front foot will bring the front toe slightly behind a line for the toes. This is also shown for the pull hitter and middleman heel line.*

After your feet are starting and moving well in relation to each other, your next question is in reference to the main direction of your stride. Is it in? Out? Parallel? Where? As you may have figured, if we are going to stride upon the heel line, the stride must go in the direction that the heel line is pointing. So the real question becomes, "How do you stand?" rather than "Where do you stride?" And again, we're back to basic style. Once you select your basic style you must then realize that the direction in which the heel line is pointing will create your general contact area and therefore dictate the area in which you will hit the ball onto the field. This is why I identify both stance and stride as distinct elements of style.

Before any confusion starts, I am not claiming that the direction of your stride is the direction in which you'll hit the ball. Remember, a pull hitter's heel line is pointing toward center field, but he's not hitting the bulk of his balls up the middle. A right-handed middle man is pointing more toward the second baseman's position, but he's hitting the majority of his balls to the middle of the field. The reason is simply because the hips have the mobility to rotate much further to the left or right (depending on your batting side) than the direction of the stride. With a right-handed hitter in mind, the relation between the direction of his stride and where the majority of his balls will be hit is much like an army tank with its nozzle stuck slightly to the left. If you line the tank up straight as shown in 5-15a, it will be shooting like a pull hitter hits; if you close or angle the tank off slightly as shown in 5-15b, it will be shooting up the middle. Please note that there's a relation between how you stand, stride and where the ball will go — and it's very important.

Certainly, I'm not saying anything new, hitters have been adjusting their feet and/or strides to direct the ball ever since the first hack. It's a natural tendency. However, it's time to take a good look at the pros and cons of these adjustments.

For example, take the guy who sets up in an even stance and then strides in like a middleman would. He's hurting himself. He is trying to open his stride leg while he steps in. Unfortunately, these clashing movements cause a poor circular headstart and its result tends to gear the hitter's swing toward outside pitches. This hitter's stance and stride is seen in Figure 5-16.

On the other hand, what about the guy who sets up as a middle man, and then steps out to an even stride? I don't like him either. Though his movement is more natural because it's on the path of the swing, he is conversely gearing himself for inside pitches. Couple stepping out with the length of the bats used today and it really makes little sense. This hitter is seen in Figure 5-17. I'm against any lateral stride movement — stay on the heel line.

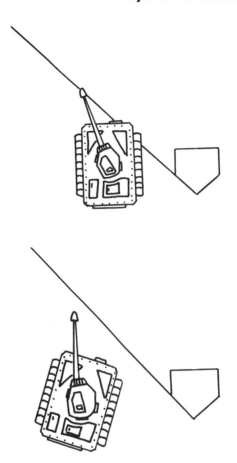

FIG 5-15 (a-b, top to bottom). *Because the hips have the ability to rotate beyond the angle of the heel line, the relation between the direction of the heel line and where the balls will be hit onto the field is much like an army tank with its nozzle pointing slightly to the left.*

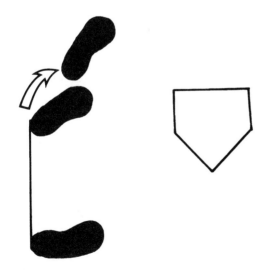

FIG 5-16. *This diagram shows the hitter who sets up in an even stance and then breaks the heel line by stepping in.*

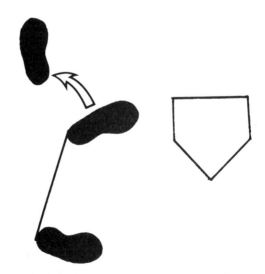

FIG 5-17. *This diagram shows the hitter who sets up in a closed stance and then breaks the heel line by stepping out.*

STYLE, STRIDE AND THE BOTTOM ARM

Yeah, I know. Pull hitter Ted Williams did not bat from an even stance, he batted from one that was slightly closed and, naturally, that goes against my basic style description of a pull hitter. Well, hear this; I don't think Ted used his arms as well as he could have. From the films and photos I've seen, he pre-extended them a little, and as I said earlier, this caused his average ball to be hit more to the right. Hey, the stories about Ted pulling the ball are endless: pulling in spite of the shift, pulling foul, and pulling into the Fenway bullpen. And while it's amazing how great a pull hitter Ted was, in my opinion, he pulled the ball too much for his own good. Ted Williams was not a natural left-hander — he threw right-handed. And while most people know that, even the best don't really understand why it is such a disadvantage. Beyond the inconvenience of not having the strongest, quickest, and most skilled arm on the top, closer to contact (which would have made Ted quicker, stronger, and more accurate), is the fact that by having his best arm on the bottom he was constantly drawn toward pre-extension. By having his doing arm (the arm that has always been most productive) on the bottom, Ted wanted to use it more than his top arm, making it very difficult for him to anchor it properly. Hey, bat from the other side someday, you'll feel what I'm talking about. It's a hard thing to deal with. To me, there's no wonder at all as to why Ted had so much trouble going to the opposite field because the swing hitters used to get the ball up the middle and to the opposite field — the inside-out stroke, which we'll talk about in a moment, requires the hitter to keep both arms bent even more at contact.

Where is all this leading to? The point is that whenever pre-extension is present, even if it's not that bad (as in Ted's case), there must be an alteration of stance and stride if the hitter is to hit the ball where he should. Ted Williams batted from a slightly closed stance to keep a reasonable percentage of his balls from going foul. What hitters must understand is that there is an important relationship between the execution of the stance, style, stride and bottom arm. The more you extend, the more you'll pull the ball and the more you'll have to close off your stance and stride to put the ball on the field where it suits you best.

As we mentioned earlier, the problem stems from the angle on which the bat will approach the ball from a pre-extended swing. Unfortunately, the only way to solve this problem is by anchoring that front arm correctly. The last thing a hitter wants to do is to accept his pre-extension and try to combat it by altering his stance and stride. This hitter is merely robbing Peter to pay Paul. A hitter like this that concedes to his pre-extension will not only have to pay its stiff and constant tolls, but will usually be forced to buy extra time with an extremely light and usually short bat.

Just as popular and twice as bad is when pre-extension dictates a hitter's style. Many times TV will feature a hitter that should clearly be a middle man, who's pulling the ball due to pre-extension. This guy is miles away from his potential. He's out of style, and he's pre-extending! What could be worse?

Not everybody is going to use their bottom arms as well as they should and therefore, although two middle men are standing and striding on the same angle, one hitter may, on the average, pull the ball a bit more; that is to say that this hitter's hitting area will be slightly more to the pull side. If Hitter A pre-extends just slightly, on the average, he will pull the ball a bit more than Hitter B. Please remember, however, that Hitter A is feeling the pains of slight pre-extension and therefore, if all talents are equal Hitter B would be the better hitter.

If Ted had been a natural lefty and did not pre-extend, he would have been even better. Mechanically, things would have been much easier for him. Had he used a longer bat and swung more efficiently, he would have hit balls harder, been quicker inside, hit fewer fouls, and hit the outside of the plate much harder. Just hitting the outside low corner more efficiently alone would have made him notably better because that's where everybody tried to pitch him. Fearing for their lives, pitchers would have started coming in on him more often (pull hitters hit a good percentage of outside pitches up the middle). Also, just due to the fact that he would not have been pulling as many balls, the shifts he faced would never have come about.

Now, don't get me wrong — I think Ted was the best. However, I don't think he was mechanically to his potential, and I'm not sure anyone ever has been to theirs. I know, how can I claim someone as great as Ted Williams had a mechanical drawback? Well, let me ask you a question for a change. "Are greats always executing to their potential?" Logic tells me that they are not. I've seen films of Willie Mays hitting, and the first thing that came to mind was how much better he could have been with better mechanics. Willie had a very long stride which placed his legs in a lesser position at crunch time. Please don't misunderstand. I'm not downing him. He may very well be the greatest all-around baseball player to ever step on the field. I just want you to know that I don't like this leave-the-guy-alone syndrome just be-

cause he's good. I think Willie Mays is a great example of someone who lost out because coaching was afraid to take a shot at helping him reach his potential. "Don't argue with success" and "Leave well enough alone" are attitudes that greats are constantly faced with. I think it stinks.

I don't think Willie was too fond of that attitude either. I saw him on a late-night talk show one time, and I detected resentment. He implied that he knew he could have been better. He said "No one ever taught me anything. They just sent me out there."

FIG 5-18. *I don't care whether a player is the next Willie Mays or the worst runt ever to lace up a pair of cleats, it is my job as a teacher to try and help each hitter to reach his potential. Here I'm marking the proper knuckle alignment on the hands of a former high school player – just a small step along the way.*

LANDING OF THE STRIDE: TIMING

There is no better time than now to begin defining another popular but misled hitting concept — *timing*. All my baseball life I've heard or read baseball authorities claim that the skillfullness in hitting a baseball was all timing, but never have I heard one of these "experts" explain exactly what they meant. What is timing? Where, when, and how do you time a pitch?

The bulk of a hitter's timing lies in his ability to get the landing of his stride (his falling forward) to jell with the speed of the anticipated pitch in such a way that will enable the hitter to "fluently" glide to his point of balance, and, if desired, continue harmoniously into his swing. The key point to remember here is that the hitter does not want to stop. The hitter should arrive to the balance point at the right time and while still in motion. The main focus in timing is this — timing the balance point. It is interesting to note that this takes place mostly in the pre-swing.

Let's face it, timing is not in the speed of your swing. I mean, you shouldn't swing faster to catch up to a fastball or slower to wait on a curve. Your swing speed is one of the few constants in hitting, and it should remain the same for all pitches. However, if both the swing speed and starting time of the stride remain consistent, how can you time different speed pitches smoothly? You know as well as I do if you were to stride and swing the same way for a curve traveling 60 miles per hour and a fast ball traveling 90 miles per hour, you would be anything but fluent. And why? Because the timing of one stride and one balance point cannot accommodate all speed pitches. Therefore, we can conclude that if the hitter wishes to swing at a given pitch from a balance point that is on time rather than a balance point that has arrived too early or late, the hitter, like the pitcher, must have the ability to fluctuate his timing, that is, to alter the arrival time of his balance point in relation to the speed he is anticipating. How is this done?

Timing your balance point is controlled by offsetting certain amounts of weight in the cocking motion to delay or advance the time in which the stride will land. For example, if I were anticipating a 60-mile-an-hour curve ball, I would bring more weight back in the cocking motion than I would if I were anticipating a 90-mile-an-hour fastball because the added offset of weight back would increase the time in which it took my body to rock or fall forward. Therefore, if I had calculated correctly, this offset of weight would then land me to my balance point while the anticipated pitch was at a distance where I could handle its speed best. Conversely, anticipating the 90-mile-an-hour pitch, I would have offset less weight back, causing my stride (my body) to fall forward sooner, enabling me to reach the balance point earlier and again while the pitch was at a distance where I could handle its speed best. By adjusting the weight distribution in the cocking motion, the hitter can advance or delay the landing of his stride and therefore time his balance point in relation to the anticipated velocity.

The movement that offsets weight in the cocking motion is the bending of the back leg. To offset weight in the cocking motion the hitter merely bends the back leg straight down to a degree that will bring the proper amount of weight back in relation to the pitch he is anticipating. This can be seen while anticipating two different speeds in Figure 5-19 (a-b).

With this in mind, we can also conclude that the size of the pendulum also fluctuates in relation to the anticipated pitch. Look at Figure 5-20 (a-b). If a hitter goes further back for a slower pitch he creates a greater swing of the pendulum. On the other hand, the anticipation of a faster pitch will produce a shorter pre-swing.

To calculate a weight shift you must have estimated and remembered about how fast the anticipated pitch was traveling. Where do you get this information? Again, you've observed. You've taken a pitch and you've questioned the hitters that have already faced the pitcher. You're taking in information and then storing it — storing it in an ongoing file of experience that eventually enables you to realize exactly how much weight you must offset to handle the different speed pitches you must face.

The smart hitter remembers not only the speeds and the timings of them, but also what pitchers throw them. By doing this, the hitter's task of day-to-day timing becomes much easier because pitchers start to fall into categories. I mean, White, Rogers, and Farley may have similar speed fastballs and/or curves, and by knowing this from past experience the smart hitter will be able to formulate a timing advantage before he ever steps into the batter's box. When he does get in the box, however, he'll still strictly observe because he knows it's very possible that "this time" the pitcher may have a little more or less on the ball or possibly even something new. What's so important here is realizing and remembering the important relationship between your observations and your timing. It's an observation followed by a preparation.

While we're on the subject, it's also important to realize that timing, and therefore observations, are personal. Just because you offset X amount of weight for a particular pitch

FIG 5-19 (a-b, left to right). *5-19a shows the anticipation of a fast pitch, 5-19b shows that of a slower pitch. Note the difference in the back knee joint controlling the backward flow.*

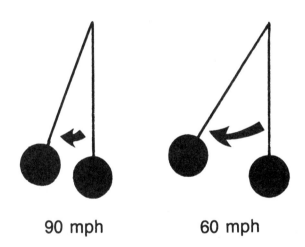

90 mph   60 mph

FIG 5-20 (a-b, left to right). *The anticipation of a slower pitch creates a greater backward and forward swing of the pendulum.*

doesn't mean that I should as well. Timing is established individually by talent. If you and I were pretty much the same except maybe you were just a bit quicker, you would offset more weight on any given pitch than I because, due to your added quickness, you could allow the ball to travel closer to you before you would have to reach your balance point. Theoretically, you would be potentially the better hitter because you would have the ability to watch the ball longer. These two hitters can be seen facing the same speed in Figure 5-21 (a-b). Hitter A, the quicker of the two, has a longer and slower pendulum motion, resulting in a balance point that arrives later than the balance point of

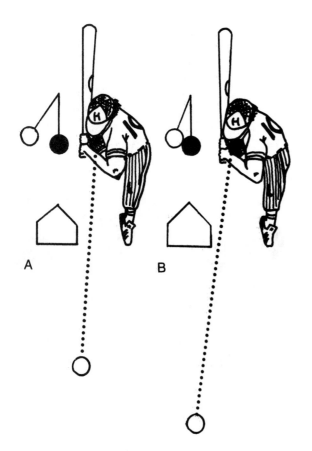

FIG 5-21 (a-b, left to right). *A hitter's talent and mechanics together will govern the average swing of the pendulum.*

Hitter B. Again, this results in the ball traveling closer to him before he must react. He has more time. Hitter B, on the other hand, has a shorter and faster pendulum motion simply because this hitter must reach his balance point sooner if he is to react in time.

Timing can also become individual due to the quality of a hitter's mechanics. Again, if our talents were equal but I pre-extended, lunged, or constantly started my stride late (it could be any number of mechanical breakdowns), I would time pitches differently than you. Much like Hitter B, I would need a balance point that arrives just a bit earlier than yours and therefore I would be forced to constantly commit my swing sooner. Due to subordinate mechanics, I would be restraining my talents.

If the individualism of timing is molded by both talent and mechanical quality, you should also be aware of another interesting fact. Even if you and I had the same visual ability, it would not necessarily mean that we were seeing the ball the same. Our eyes judge speed only in relation to our personal reaction ability. A hitter's ability to see the ball is formulated by vision, talent and mechanical quality. Did Ted Williams have the greatest eyes in baseball? Probably not! Did he have the greatest combination? I wouldn't doubt it. With this in mind, whenever you ask a fellow player about the speed of a pitch, have him compare it to another pitch and/or pitcher. You should do this because answers like "He's fast," or "He's slow," may be way off base through your eyes. Always gain that sort of information by comparison.

When you have a feel for offsetting weight properly, the only other ingredients required for good timing are starting the stride on time and receiving the pitch you anticipated. I call these three elements the *timing triangle*, which is no

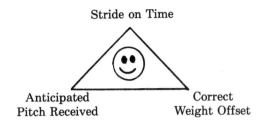

FIG 5-22. *This simple diagram, "The Timing Triangle", is a reminder of what it takes to achieve proper timing.*

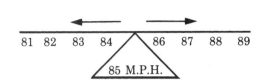

FIG 5-23. *A certain offsetting of weight will cover a short range of speeds slower or faster than perfection.*

more than a simple model that hopefully will remind hitters what it takes to be on time. This model can be seen in Figure 5-22.

Obviously, each positive triangle — each correct offset of weight — will cover a certain range of pitch speeds that you can handle fluently. I mean, you don't have two separate triangles for 90 and 91 miles per hour. There's a span here, and though I am still not sure of its size, it certainly exists and you must realize that. For learning purposes, if we imagine the span to be 9 miles per hour, what I'm claiming is that an offset of weight geared ideally for 85 miles per hour will cover any speed slower or faster than 85 miles per hour up to a 4-mile-per-hour range in either direction. Therefore, an offset of weight ideally for 85 miles per hour will cover the range of 81 to 89 miles per hour. This can be seen in Figure 5-23.

TIMING FEEL

It is now also easier to understand the clue of timing feel. Timing feel is just realizing from the flight of the ball whether or not you're getting the speed you anticipated. Timing feel simply tells you if your timing is on or off. Your timing feel provides any one of three different feelings, all of which have different meanings: 1) it can feel good when you've timed and an-

ticipated the correct speed; 2) it can feel like you're very early when you get a pitch traveling slower than expected; and 3) it can feel like you're very late when you get a pitch that's faster than you expected. A good hitter must be able to recognize how he feels and know immediately what to do from that point. Hey, if you've got less than two strikes and here comes a pitch right down the pipe, but your timing feel is telling you you're late, — you should take that pitch! But many hitters will go right after that ball and stupidly pop it up simply because they don't understand or utilize the importance of timing feel.

You know, ever since you've been little, a good ball to hit has solely been described by location. A good pitch was over the plate about crotch high. But as you grow up that changes. It is my feeling that timing outweighs location. Provided the hitter has the right bat in his hands, a pitch that is not timed will do him in much quicker than a timed pitch in a tough location. This is why I have suggested conceding location when you're outmatched by a real tough pitcher. It's only sensible to cling to your timing, because you still have your balance and your stride momentum on your side. Sure, we want good location too, but to concede timing for location, like the hitter I just described, is asinine.

FIG 5-24. *The hitter pictured above is shown at the point of his stride where he is experiencing "timing feel." Here, he is processing information about the incoming pitch and using speed as his first important clue.*

THE STRIDE'S LENGTH AND HEIGHT

Stride length also deserves some thought. How far should you stride? Is it two inches? Six inches? Two feet? Many times I hear coaches claim that good hitters have short strides and while I agree, I feel the topic contains some blanks to be filled. For example, what exactly are we measuring? And most important, how do you find the correct stride length for you? As far as I'm concerned, the length of the stride is the distance that the stride heel has traveled on the heel line from the stance. This distance is seen in Figure 5-25. Although the toe has rotated much further, one should be concerned with the movement that brings the hitter toward balance. This movement is the forward movement of the pendulum and is best measured by the stride heel's progression.

Good hitters use their timing feel effectively. If they don't get what they're looking for they don't swing. If their timing feel reads early or late they shut themselves off; The message is No — no swing. On the other hand, if the timing feel reads good then they'll continue to sort additional information (location, color, spin), which may or may not render a swing.

If you think about it, timing is where all the pieces start coming together. I mean, up until now you've been creating speed and strength through good mechanical execution but now, through observation and calculation, you're bringing the advantages you've created to the point (in relation to a given pitch) where they can be used most effectively. The hitter's ongoing goal is putting a solid swing on time. How does he do it? Observation, calculation and pre-swing! It is here where the entire hitter is tested, and it is here where most of the beauty of pain of the skill is encountered.

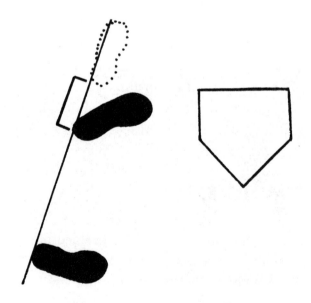

FIG 5-25. *The length of the stride should be measured by the front heel's progression along the heel line.*

The length of your stride is individual and will depend upon both the length of your legs and your flexibility. The best way to find stride length is to ask yourself this question: "Is my stride bringing me to my balance point with my legs positioned properly?" ("Is my front leg landing toe first? Is my front knee still bent? Is my back leg still bent as it was in the cocking motion?") If the answer to these questions is "Yes," then you have found good stride length. I have found that good leg positioning usually drops the stride at a distance that is less than the length of the hitter's foot. For example, my foot is 11+ inches long and I stride about 6 to 7 inches.

As you might suspect, stride length problems are: 1) reaching out with the front knee; or 2) straightening out the back leg. If either of these movements occur during the stride, the stride's distance will increase, causing the hitter to land in a poor position for good hip rotation. The effect of these tendencies can be seen in Figure 5-26 (a-b).

Very rarely does anybody address the height of the stride, but it is also important. I believe in a low stride. In the outfield grass this stride would remain in touch with the grass throughout the entire movement. I like a low stride because, until the stride leg lands, the hitter is missing a good portion of his swing. Remember, that leg represents power and speed; without that leg on the ground, you've got nothing. Why would anybody want to prolong its flight by lifting it up higher — bringing it further from its critical destination? I have found high striding many times to be a hitter's solution to his fear of striding on time. When you merely lift the stride leg up, your body really isn't going anywhere. The hitter is trying to move without making any commitment — he's trying to move and remain safe. High striding is no more than a camouflaged late stride (Figure 5-27).

FIG 5-26 (a-b, left to right). *If the front or back knee extends prematurely, the stride will be lengthened and a poor landing position will result.*

FIG 5-27. *High striding is a common way of dealing with the fear of starting forward early. These hitters are all late and in my opinion not really striding at all. Remember, a stride is a controlled headstart involving the entire body.*

FIG 5-28. *Former Boston Red Sox star Wade Boggs (a middle man by choice) drives a pitch to left center from a slightly closed stance. Boggs, himself a student of hitting and reader of* The Science of Hitting *as a young player, is great from the neck up. I believe that this particular photo shows that his eyes are leaving at a pretty good point. However, I'm still not wild about Boggs' choice of the middle man hitting style.*

Timing and the Strike Zone

Let's take a closer look at the term *contact area*. Your contact area is a three-dimensional area, as high and wide as your strike zone, with a depth that is measured by the distance between its two most extreme contact points. These points are illustrated below — the high inside strike in Figure 6-1a and the low outside strike in Figure 6-1b. Figure 6-1c illustrates the contact area's depth.

Your contact area holds a specific position in relation to both your body and the pitcher's release point. Holding off on the singles hitter, in Figure 6-2 we see the relation between style, the pitcher's release point and the position of the contact area. Due to the slightly closed stance of the two middle men they will contact all their pitches further from the pitcher's re-

lease point. This hitter's stance and stride has moved his entire contact area back toward the catcher, therefore providing him with the extra time we spoke of earlier.

Also in Figure 6-2 note that while the contact area can be moved in relation to the pitcher by stance and stride, it should not move in relation to the hitter's body. In both styles the outside and low pitch is being contacted at a point or depth about perpendicular to the instep of the front foot, while the high inside strike is being hit out in front of the body.

To hit the locations of the strike zone consistently and with authority, the hitter must strive to hit each location at its own specific depth in the contact area. Though a difficult task, the ongoing attempt to meet the different

FIG 6-1 (a-c, left to right). *The strike zone has an element of depth that I find more significant than both its width and height. 6-1a displays the contact point of one extreme, the high and inside pitch, while 6-1b displays the other extreme, the low and outside pitch. 6-1c displays the entire depth as measured between these two extremes.*

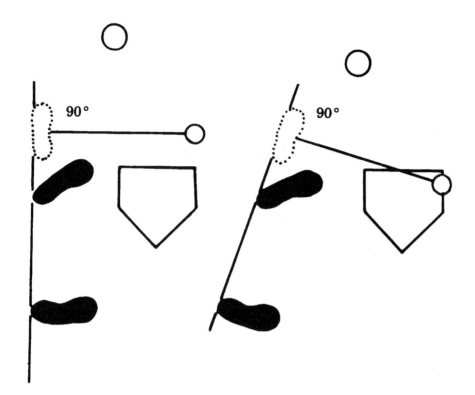

locations properly will help build and maintain a mechanical and visual anchor point, from which the entire zone can be approached consistently. When a hitter neglects to hit his strike zone locations at their respective points, he is changing his swing! He is adopting new mechanics to handle certain locations. For example, many hitters when facing an outside strike will come forward (lunge) as opposed to waiting for it and hitting it correctly at its proper depth. By altering their mechanics these hitters have changed their swing speeds along with their visual anchor point. These hitters are using two different swings and two different viewpoints. As you might guess, these hitters experience their share of timing problems because two of their hitting constants, swing speed and vision, are now changing with location.

So you hit different locations at different depths, but how do you get the bat to them properly and at what depths are these locations hit? The bat is brought to different depths of the con-

tact area by rotating the hips to a suitable degree. With a closer look at our contact area extremes, we can see not only the relationship of hip rotation to the contact points, but also the relationship between the strike zone locations and their contact area depth. As you can see in Figure 6-1a, the high inside strike is not only the pitch that will be contacted closest to the pitcher, but also the pitch that requires the most movement — the greatest amount of hip rotation. Due to the length of the rotation and the location of contact in relation to the pitcher's release point, the up and in pitch leaves the hitter with the least amount of time. Keep in mind, however, that due to the momentum created, this area is hit hardest. The low and away pitch is just the opposite. It is contacted furthest from the pitcher, requires the least amount of rotation, and therefore provides the hitter with the greatest amount of time. However, due to a lack of momentum, this area is hit the weakest. This can be seen in Figure 6-1b.

FIG 6-3 & 6-4 (left to right). *Using my reaction intensity graph, strike zone locations can take their rightful place within the depth of the strike zone.*

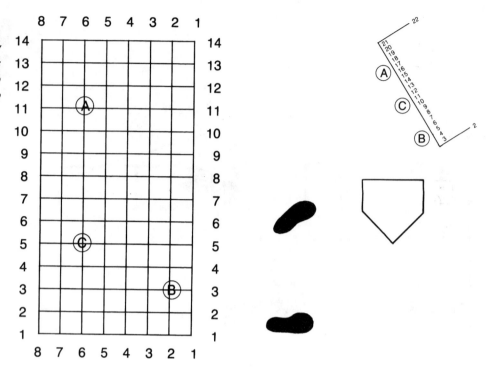

With the characteristics of the extreme locations in mind, take a look at Figure 6-3. Here you see a strike zone surrounded by numbers, numbers that are increasing in value when traveling up or in; and decreasing when traveling down or away. After finding and adding the height and width numbers from any location in the strike zone, we have ourselves a number that represents two things: 1) the reaction intensity of the swing — the amount of hip rotation necessary to reach the contact point; and 2) the placement of a strike zone location to a specific depth in the contact area. For example, Pitch A on this diagram, with a height of 11 and width of 6, has the high reaction intensity of 17 (22 and 2 are the extremes).

Shifting to Figure 6-4, we see a scale that converts reaction intensity to a depth in the contact area. And in this case, due to the high reaction intensity of 17, Point A is contacted fairly early on the scale (closer to the pitcher). Conversely, Point B, with a height of 3 and a width of 2, has a low reaction intensity of 5 and therefore, because it requires less hip action, it is contacted later or deeper on the scale (further from the pitcher). Point C, which has a reaction intensity of 11 (an intensity exactly between our high of 17 and low of 5), will be contacted at a depth exactly between the two within the contact area as well.

By creating this numbered strike zone graph, I have designed a model to help the student understand the three-dimensional relationship between these important elements of hitting: the batter's hip rotation, the different strike zone locations, and the depth in which those locations must be met for mechanical consistency at the plate.

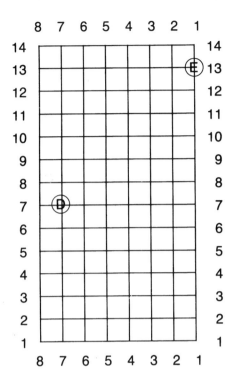

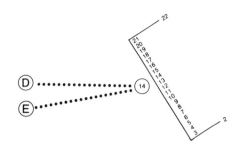

FIG 6-5 & 6-6 (left to right). *The reaction intensity graph can also help us realize how different locations can and should be contacted at the same depths.*

A closer look reveals the fact that regardless of strike zone location, if the reaction intensity numbers are equal in value, they will be hit at the same depth, with the same amount of hip action. For example, in Figures 6-5 and 6-6, though Points D and E are in separate strike zone locations, they will be hit at the same depth in the contact area.

A step further, in Figures 6-7 and 6-8, I have divided your field area into three separate zones. These zones have then been labeled with a range of reaction intensities. The idea is to show (with less than two strikes) where the different strike zone locations should be hit on the field when executing with good mechanics. The feedback you get from understanding where different pitch locations should be hit on the field is a must for the creation and consistent use of a sound swing in style.

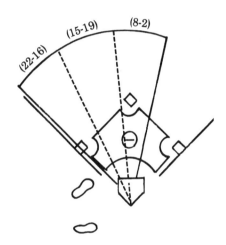

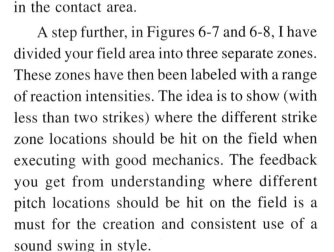

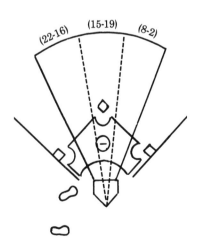

FIG 6-7 & 6-8 (top to bottom). *Here, we see where the different reaction intensities should be hit onto the field. Understanding where the different strike zone locations should be hit is important feedback.*

105

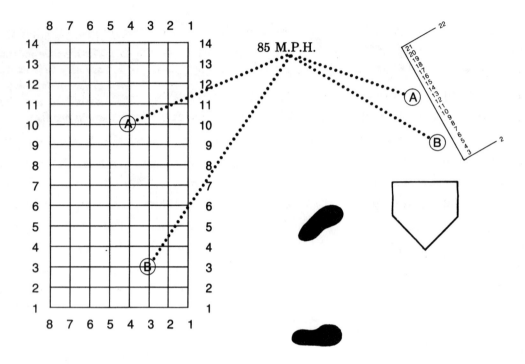

FIG 6-9. *The above diagram shows how two separate 85-mph pitches are really traveling at different speeds when viewed through the reaction intensity graph perspective. The hitter who understands these details will have a greater advantage at the plate.*

STARTING THE SWING: TRIGGER TIMING FROM THE GLIDE

After understanding where, when, and how different locations are contacted, you can easily understand that although two pitches are traveling at the same speed, a difference in location may change their speed when viewed through the eyes of *reaction intensity*. For example, in Figure 6-9, although Pitches A and B are both traveling at 85 miles per hour, Pitch A has a reaction intensity of 14, while Pitch B only has a reaction intensity of 6. Pitch A is a faster pitch due to its location and contact point. Because the majority of locations are contacted at different depths, the strike zone possesses a slight timing of its own.

When a hitter establishes a familiarity with the strike zone's timing, he is then ready to reap the benefits of what I call *trigger timing*. Now, trigger timing is no more than starting your swing — pulling the trigger or popping the hips at the right time in relation to the ball's location. After a timing feel that reads on time, and if the pitch is in the general area desired (boxes), the hitter will continue to track the pitch and then swing the fat part of his bat through the assumed contact point at a predicted point in time. This is the final timing stage of hitting and everything that has been written in this book has been to make this easier. The hitter can not see the contact point and he is not sure exactly where it is. Only consistency of approach will allow the hitter to make strong predictions on a day-to-day basis.

Trigger timing can be the difference between good and fair contact. I mean, if the ball's in the anticipated area and your pre-swing and glide place your balance point on time, you should make contact. However, if you want to start converting a greater percentage of hit balls into screamers, you must start to understand and deal with timing on its fine tuning stage. For example, let's say the count is one-and-one and you're looking for a fastball, even area; sure enough, your timing feel reads good and here it comes; but it's on the low outside corner of your even area. Many hitters will be a hair quick on that ball and ground it out. (When you're "early" with a slight upswing, you will hit the "top of the ball — on the other hand, if you're "late" you'll hit the "bottom"). But the hitter who understands the timing within his strike zone knows that pitch is really a bit slower, and therefore he will continue his glide and delay his commitment just a hair. How is this done?

Trigger timing is the hitter's prediction of, and arrival to, the contact point. To do this, first on the list is to know the hip rotation required for each strike zone location and where they should be hit on the field in relation to your style! These are your contact points — if you don't know them, you can't create them. Now I don't think you have to go through all of them daily, but I do think you need to know these five intimately. Up and in, up and away, down and in, low and away, and right down the middle. I call this the *five on dice*. If you do not understand the hip rotation, the contact depth and the place on the field where these balls should be hit in your basic style, you will never reach potential. The next step is to practice them and I'll go over several drills for this later.

So now the pitch is on its way and every thing feels on time, you continue tracking the pitch in your glide, you predict a contact point. But the ball is just not there yet! Or maybe the ball is closer than anticipated! The position of the pitch and the balance point are not going to match perfectly. What do you do?

Do you know what is hard about writing this book? Trying to write it in a manner that is not confusing. To do this, I've had to hold information until the appropriate place where it fits best. This is one of those times. When the hitter first lands his stride, he is not quite to balance! This is why the hitter's landing should be relatively soft. After the hitter lands he will start "the glide" as previously discussed. During the glide the hitter will then reach balance and uncage the swing.

What is important is that the glide allows the hitter a little extra time to read the pitch while still in motion. Equally important, and the solution to the problem above, is that the hitter can control or time the balance point during the glide. A hitter who is slightly late can gently thrust himself to balance with a slight gas peddle type push from the back foot. Not the knee, but the back foot — the ankle joint. On the other side of timing, the hitter who is slightly early can delay the balance point by slowing down the glide with resistance from the front knee and the ball of the front foot. These movements are too slight to photograph — just inches. On the same line if the hitter above is not that late or that early, he is going to hit the ball.

To put this in perspective, I'm talking about the timing difference between a hard ground ball and a line drive or between a fly ball and a line drive. Only a hitter who has met the requirements of the timing triangle can expect to experiment with controlling the balance point in the glide. This is not a system for timing, but rather, a fine tuning tool within one.

If a hitter does not execute the basics of timing, offsetting weight and striding on time, he will never experience this. For example, hitters who are late with their strides usually do not land properly or reach the balance point at all. The only thing they have control over is the upper body and that's just how they swing. Another example is the hitter who is always too early for the curve ball. Most times he'll come way beyond the balance point and destroy everything. Both of these hitters are miles away from what I'm talking about.

Now, I realize that controlling the balance point sounds like a tough task. You may think I'm getting too complicated with all this talk of timing, but I'm not. With good mechanics, you won't believe how much information you can absorb and react to. Don't sell yourself short!

Trigger timing becomes more difficult as the boxes get bigger and it is important to realize

this. While it is true that most times the hitter will hit in the even area, understanding the three dimensions of the strike zone, and how they relate to timing, can be a real motivator toward a hitter working the count. If possible, the hitter wants to do everything he can to bring the count to the rip area because through the eyes of timing it is the easiest area to hit in.

Figure 6-10 shows a rip area and Figure 6-11 shows an even area; Figure 6-12 shows the difference in depth and timing responsibilities of these two areas. The larger the box area the more balls there are to hit. But keep in mind that as the hitting area grows it becomes progressively more difficult to pull the trigger at the right time. Figures 6-13 and 6-14 show why it is important to look for pitches in the middle of your boxes. The hitter cannot make extreme trigger adjustments. We are playing the average location of each box — the middle.

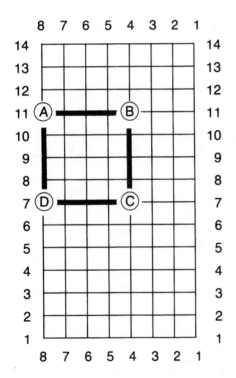 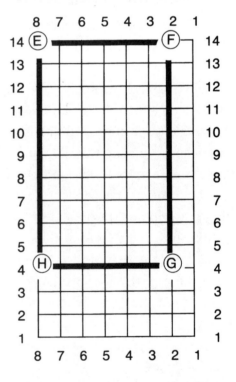

FIG 6-10 & 6-11. *The reaction intensity chart can also help us to see the timing requirements of the different hitting areas. Rip area (A-D) is compared to even area (E-H) in Figure 6-12.*

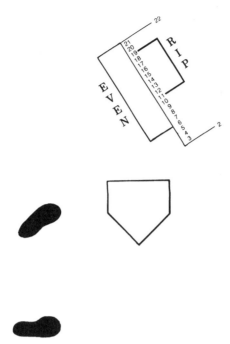

FIG 6-12. *Rip areas and even areas not only grow in width and height but also in depth. The bigger the area, the more balls that it will be necessary to time.*

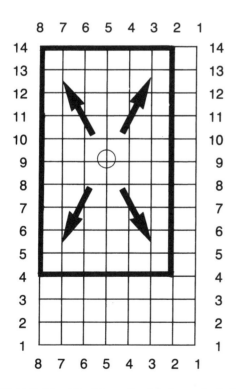

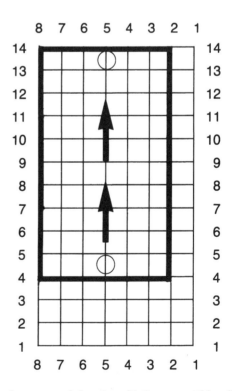

FIG 6-13 & 6-14. *The hitter should always look for the pitch within the center of the given hitting area. This will allow slight trigger timing adjustments to be made with much less difficulty as seen in 6-13. In 6-14 the extreme trigger timing adjustment for an even area pitch that was anticipated low and arrived high is shown.*

FIG 6-15. *I cannot say enough about the importance of understanding strike zone depth. Multitudes of players simply don't understand where the different strike zone locations should be hit in relation to the playing field nor do they recognize that the position of the hitter's body at the plate is equally important. Take a look at the opening shot to this chapter – the classic photo of Ted Williams and his strike zone. That photo means so much to me it's like an old friend. My work has come a long way since reading The Science of Hitting and discussing the art of hitting with Ted Williams. I'm confident that the information in this chapter will give players and coaches a stronger foothold on understanding the difficulties of timing.*

Other Strokes

THE INSIDE-OUT STROKE

The inside-out stroke is a shorter swing designed for contact. Its qualities make it not only the ideal swing for the singles hitter, but also for any hitter with two strikes or facing a slump. By setting the hitter's contact area further back in relation to his body as shown in Figure 7-1, the inside-out stroke enhances contact percentages by simply providing the hitter with more decision time.

Its main mechanical difference is that the arms and wrists never fully extend. This in turn creates a shorter swing, a swing with a lessened range of motion, making the hitter not only quicker but more accurate. By not extending the arms and wrists fully the bat will now trail or be parallel to the hands at contact.

FIG 7-1. *The inside-out stroke brings the bat through the zone with the barrel trailing the hands. The wrists and arms do not extend fully making it a shorter quicker stroke.*

FIG 7-2. *Due to the position of the arms and wrists at contact when using the inside-out stroke, balls will be hit to the plate side of the heel line. The tank nozzle is now slightly to the plate side.*

Because the arms and wrists are bent the bat will now contact the strike zone locations from a new angle. Due to this, our previous relationship between where the ball is located in the strike zone and where it will be hit onto the field changes. The balls will now be hit to the plate side of the heel line. Now, it is as if the army tank is shooting just slightly to the right on a right-handed batter (Figure 7-2).

WITH TWO STRIKES

How is the inside-out stroke used with two strikes? When a hitter finds himself with two strikes the fight for time becomes amplified. Not only is the hitter facing his largest area (the entire strike zone), but he also must now sacrifice the aid of anticipating one certain pitch. To combat these problems the hitter must be able to react as quickly as possible. Therefore, when a hitter gets his second strike, several other adjustments should be made along with the use of the inside-out stroke. The hitter should: 1) level off his bat; 2) choke up, or even better, switch bats to a lighter model with an identical length; 3) move closer to the plate; 4) concentrate on hitting the ball up the middle — that is, hitting the ball in the same area that the middle men do normally; 5) open up the stance and stride; and 6) move the target area to *the white*.

Now you may give me flack for recommending an open stance, but think about it. What is the main adjustment in making a stroke quicker and shorter? It's a reduction in hip rotation. The more rotation, the longer the stroke; the longer the stroke, the more time you need to bring the barrel to contact. With two strikes, we want to shorten the distance between the barrel of the bat and the contact point. This is done best by opening the stance slightly before we even start. One should also note that because the ball is directed away from the hitter with the inside-out stroke, opening up also becomes a necessity for hitting the ball up the middle. These adjustments can be seen in Figure 7-3 (a-c).

When a hitter gets two strikes, he can no longer guess. There's no taking a pitch with a wrong guess now. Your back is to the dugout. Therefore, when a hitter receives two strikes, he must prepare his pre-swing for the pitcher's mid-speed pitch. That is to say, if a guy has three pitches, one traveling at 60 mph, one at 70 mph, and one at 80 mph, you'd prepare for the 70 mph pitch because that timing makes either of the other two pitches an easier adjustment. With two strikes we are coming to the balance point at a time that will enable us to adjust to the pitcher's extremes (one should note that this sort of adjusting can only occur successfully with the two-strike stroke). If the pitcher doesn't have a mid-speed pitch, the hitter imagines one. For example, if the pitcher had a fastball that traveled at about 80 mph and a curve ball at 60 mph, you'd imagine and prepare for a pitch at 70 mph.

Why hit the ball up the middle with two strikes? Well, first and foremost, when hitting up the middle you have a greater chance of making contact because more of the bat is in the potential contact area for a longer period of time than in both the pull or opposite field strokes. Looking at the field, the middle is the largest area because most times center field is much deeper. Here, there are fewer foul balls along with a wide spectrum of difficult plays for the shortstop, second baseman and pitcher. Using the shortened two-strike swing I've suggested, all hitters can and must take advantage.

In closing, a hitter should note that reaching potential will rest to some degree on his two-strike execution. Solid two-strike hitting enables a hitter to be confident and selective before two strikes. A hitter who is afraid to be under the gun has the tendency to open up his rip and even areas early in the count, when he could be taking his chances on the next pitch.

FIG 7-3 (a-c, left to right). *Photo sequence (a-c) displays the two-strike adjustments: a leveled bat, an opened stance with the back foot closer to the plate, and hitting to the middle of the field with a higher target area in your sights.*

TWO-STRIKE TARGET AREA

Using the inside-out stroke the arm and wrist execution will cause the barrel of the bat to trail or be parallel to the hands during contact. Because of this the barrel of the bat tends to be below the hands at contact. This can be seen in Figure 7-4. Due to this fact the hitter must raise his sights when using the inside-out stroke. It can vary from *the white* to *over the white*. It will depend on how you use your arms and wrists.

FIG 7-4. *Because the barrel of the hitter's bat travels behind the hands in the inside-out stroke, the barrel will be lower than the hands at contact. Here it is important that the hitter raise his sights.*

COBB'S SPLIT GRIP

I called Ted Williams the number one forefather of technical hitting and he is, but he is not the only forefather. One of my best students ever, Roger Snow, came up to me one day in camp and asked — have you ever taken a serious look at the split grip? He then explained why he thought it was in line with Ted's basic beliefs! After five years of study I think Roger is correct and I believe that there is much merit in Ty Cobb's split grip. Its arms are just as short as the two-strike stroke and it is very quick. It is also much stronger at contact. It feels odd until you've done it a bit and I cannot say at this point that I would advocate using it before two strikes. (Maybe as a singles hitter.) But it can get the fat part of the bat to the ball quicker and stronger. It taps into the lead arm for speed and power.

The movements are like that of sweeping a broom toward you. If you look at Figure 7-5a you will see I am sweeping an upside down broom. In Figure 7-5b the movements come to life as I sweep an imaginary wall. Now, notice that in Figure 7-5c the bat is level to my hands more like a customary stroke. Due to this fact, the split grip requires no target area adjustment. This alone makes it interesting.

FIG 7-5 (a-c, left to right). *Cobb's split grip adds speed and power by tapping into the front arm as a power source. This grip should feel as though you are sweeping a wall on the plate side of your body.*

THE SINGLES HITTER

Understanding the inside-out stroke, you can see why the singles hitter, the true runner, should always use it. Remember, his most significant physical talent is his footspeed, and he would be crazy to jeopardize not making contact as consistently with a longer stroke. Hitting the ball harder but contacting it less is not in the best interest of his ability, especially when he's on the turf.

With two strikes the singles hitter's adjustments is only setting up for the mid-speed pitch. The singles hitter should be the best two-strike hitter of the four styles. He is using this stroke all the time. He is a master at it.

However, due to the nature of his style, the singles hitter will not face as many two-strike situations. Again, the tendency is for pitchers to go right at him. As a result, the singles hitter must guard against being overaggressive.

Interesting to note is that in a sense, *all styles become single hitters with two strikes.* All styles must concede to the pitcher with a stroke geared toward quick, solid contact to all strike zone locations.

OPPOSITE FIELD HITTING

What about going to the opposite field in order to move runners? For this I recommend using what Ted called his *left field stride.* Here Ted backed off the plate and closed off his stance. Then, using his arms as described with the inside-out stroke, he would stride into the ball (like a middle man normally would) and direct it to left field. This can be seen in Figure 7-6 where a right-handed batter displays the stroke.

FIG 7-6. *The opposite field stride coupled with the inside-out arm position is the only true solution for hitting the other way. Again, the hitter should raise his sights. This is natural for the middle man but much more of a task for the pull hitter and singles hitter.*

Much like described in the Ted Williams model, I recommend that all styles close off just slightly when your job at the plate is to take the pitch to the opposite field. However, I don't believe that the average hitter must close off as much as Williams himself did. When trying to go the other way, again the slight pre-extension of Ted's top arm forced him to close off a bit more. After striding, Ted's back toe would line up with his front heel. You, however, should not have to close off any more than the slightly closed stance I described for the middle man. A representation of these stance positions can be seen in Figure 7-7 (a-b).

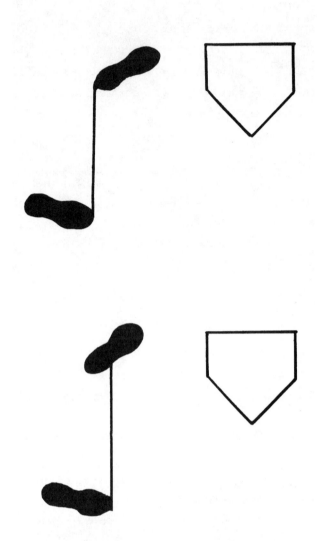

FIG 7-7 (a-b, top to bottom). *Often when asked to go the other way with the ball, players will close the stance off to an extreme (heel to toe) as shown in 7-7a. I don't think this is a good idea. For one, a good catcher will often see what you are up to and pepper you inside. On the average, I don't feel that a hitter should have to close off more than the slightly closed stance of the middle man as shown in 7-7b. Let the arms arms and wrists move the ball for you.*

Keep in mind that you may not have to back off the plate. While it's true that Ted backed off it's important to realize that many times he was doing it to beat the Boudreau shift. (The Boudreau shift was a defensive maneuver that stacked the third baseman, shortstop, and center fielder on the right side of the diamond where Ted was known to hit the ball. Hoping he would hit into the shift, Ted was pitched inside.) Naturally, by backing off the plate it became easier for him to deal with this new crop of inside pitches. What I'm getting at is the fact that most players are not facing shifts, and therefore standing off the plate may not be to your advantage. For example, if you're a powerful middle man with a man on first, facing a normal defense, and the hit-and-run sign, your ability to hit the long ball may cause the battery to pitch you away. Naturally, if you're off the plate like Ted was you'll be forced to reach. A hitter's distance from the plate in an opposite field situation depends on how the pitcher has pitched him in the past.

Opposite field hitting reminds me of something else worthy of discussion. Ted talked about closing off as a way to gain time, claiming that when you close off your stance you keep setting your contact points further from the pitcher's release point. Naturally, I agree. We've already talked about that. Many times however, I'm asked why I don't advocate hitters closing off their stance with two strikes. Why not go to the opposite field more so than up the middle? Though the opposite field swing can provide an increase in decision time, it can not bring the hitter to all strike zone locations effectively. Try this. Position yourself in the box so that you can reach the outside corner with inside-out arm execution and the opposite field stride. Do you think you can hit the inside pitch? I can't. The inside pitch becomes murder, while inside and low becomes next to impossible. With two strikes we've got to set up in such a way that will cover all locations. It just can't be done as well with the opposite field stroke.

Mechanically speaking the reason is that the angle of the stride clashes with the deepened contact area. Remember, regardless of the type of swing you're using, the hips have got to lead the way. They've got to clear out for the arms and bat! When standing at a distance that would enable you to reach the outside corner and supposedly all pitches from there in, my point comes to life. When positioned like this, the hitter seems to run out of hip rotation before the bat can reach the inside contact points. The

result is an upper body swing with a loss of speed and power. Think about it, if we want to reach further, be quicker, and clear the hips, we have got to get closer and shorten the swing and this can be done best by moving closer and opening up.

I know, now you're going to argue that Ted Williams used the opposite field stroke with two strikes. I'm not going to argue with that. I'm sure he did. But he had good reason to. First and foremost the short left field wall at Fenway, and equally in his favor his reputation as a power pull hitter. When Ted wasn't facing the shift, I'd bet he did not back off the plate because without the shift the tendency was to keep it away from him. Without the shift Ted's pull with power reputation decreased the amount of inside two-strike pitches he faced, therefore enabling him to go the other way with something on it.

FIG 7-8. *Here the hitter is shown in the slightly open, two-strike position. The back foot is closer than normal and the heel line is heading toward shortstop.*

FIG 7-9. *Here the trailing barrel of the inside-out stroke is shown. Notice that the bat barrel is slightly behind the hands and slightly lower than the hands. The overall contact point is much deeper in the zone – deeper in relation to the hitter's body and his stroke before two strikes.*

Did Ted play it smart as a hitter? Sure he did. As a matter of fact he provides a great example of individual style; however, it is individual! When it's Ted Williams at Fenway Park — great! But on the average, most hitters would be losing out adopting that sort of two-strike leverage. The opposite field stroke is longer, it takes more time, and therefore, again, it's not as accurate as the two-strike position I've suggested. Closing off also starts the barrel of the bat further from contact, and I'll tell you something else, with two strikes I don't like the angle on which it brings the bat's barrel into contact. Opened up you'll have more bat surface to hit with and more bat in the contact area for a longer period of time.

FIG 7-10. *The angle of the stride with the "inside-out execution" of the arms and wrists becomes not only the ideal combination for pushing the ball to the middle of the field, but also for keeping the greatest amount of hitting surface in the potential contact area. Both of these points come alive as a ball is pushed to right center from an open stance and plenty of bat in the zone. (To help drive this point home, imagine a hitter using his arms and wrists as he would in a normal stroke but from an open stance – he would have to pull almost everything with a high percentage of those pitches being pulled foul. This would also produce a very limited hitting surface at contact.)*

Practice

Another factor that makes hitting so hard is practicing it correctly. To practice correctly, you need a list of things; you need a pitcher or a machine, decent baseballs, bats, a mound, a decent backstop and playable weather. And unfortunately, even if you've got all these things, often it's still not enough. For example: the pitcher has got to throw at the speed you'll be seeing and with proper control. You can't practice when only every fifth pitch is a strike or if you're constantly worried about getting drilled. What about all those holes in the batter's box? You can't practice when the local box has two 5 inch cleat holes the size of a bread box. Those holes can cause a hitter to stand and stride off balance. The box should be level, and that's important. We can't forget the cost of baseballs; or even worse, losing them. You go down to the field (if there is one) with that one friend who never says, "No," and you start throwing to one another; and before you know it, you've got balls going everywhere. You know what I mean; it's like they're trying to escape. Good baseballs are expensive. You've got to have a

mound; that's imperative. If you throw off level ground, the ball will approach the hitter on a different angle, drastically distorting your feedback. A fly-out on flat ground may be a line shot off a mound. Don't forget that. How about the weather? You can't use baseballs very efficiently in wet weather; you need something that won't pick up the water. I have found those hard machine balls with the stitches to work best, but you still need someone to throw them. (You can't use a machine in the rain). Naturally, nobody will throw in the rain — rain is a throwing repellent! Whether it's pitching batting practice or just throwing in general, when it rains and/or the temperature drops a bit, it seems as though everybody is suddenly haunted with the fear of a potential arm injury. You'd think everybody was under a multimillion-dollar contract — too much care, not enough dare. It's really kind of funny watching a high school player who can't field a fly ball to save his mother's life shift into a protective and reluctant attitude with the first sign of rain. What puppies.

FIG 8-1. *Every time a young man says he wants to play for me I make sure he knows exactly what that entails. I tell the player that I am the nicest but toughest guy they are ever going to meet. Why do I do this? Because to me a good coach provides a realistic reflection of life – he fights to represent it truthfully. In life there are no successful puppies... Here, I explain to Riccardo Santiago why I thought he did a great job this past summer.*

FIG 8-2. *Live hitting is the ultimate practice situation. It utilizes style, timing, tunneling, swing execution, and the two-strike stroke. But... the challenge of finding quality live hitting practice is another story.*

MENTAL AND PHYSICAL

Live Hitting

When and if you finally get everything right, the big question is how do you practice. Well, if you're a mature hitter — if you can swing, guess at incoming pitches and make the necessary corrections — I recommend live practice as much as possible; that is, I suggest hitting outdoors, against a pitcher throwing off a mound and with a catcher calling a live, game-situation count. We're not talking 1-and-1 or two-strike counts but 0-and-0, just like it would be if you were to step up to the plate in a real game. While practicing, the hitter should pay strict attention to where and how the ball is being hit in relation to both where the pitch was in the strike zone and how much weight he had to offset in his pre-swing. Also, the hitter should

question any call made by the catcher (catcher umpires) that didn't seem correct from the hitter's point of view. Remember, the catcher has a better vantage point from which to judge the pitch, so a hitter can use his observations to help understand exactly where pitches are crossing the plate.

In a live practice session, the pitcher must be trying to get the hitter out. This is why I like to see live practice in a competitive atmosphere. The mature hitter should always practice under pressure. This is where I think betting is great. Bet against your buddies for a pizza. If money is a problem, bet on sit-ups or sprints. When there's something to lose, you'll try harder. There's pressure in a game; and I feel a mature hitter must practice not just his hitting, but his hitting as he deals with pressure. If you take the pressure out of a mature hitter's practice, you won't be doing him any favors.

Whiffle Ball

If there is something that is helpful to hitting — something easy to do, safe, competitive, weather friendly, space conscious and cheap — it is whiffle ball. Once a hitter knows a thing or two about hitting, whiffle ball, when played correctly, can really fill some voids. First and foremost, a whiffle ball thrown correctly will break much sharper than a baseball giving the hitter plenty of tunneling practice on the breaking ball. Second, it provides for a ton of at-bats. This fall we played a ten-game season of six inning games one-on-one. I averaged about five plate appearances an inning, that's 30 a game and a total of 300 plate appearances, not counting the playoffs. I averaged about three pitches per at-bat — that's roughly 900 pitches. I other words I tunneled 900 pitches this fall in competition. If you're a high school player playing a twenty-game schedule, maybe you'll average 80 plate appearances per season. You'll tunnel maybe 240 pitches. Get the idea?

In order to gain any benefit from such practice, however, you have to play correctly. We use two different whiffle ball types in our various drills. One is an all-holed ball, which is much easier to control but breaks very little; it is used to represent the fastball. The other is a half-holed ball, which is harder to control and breaks a great deal. The pitcher keeps each type of ball hidden in his pocket or pouch and may choose to throw either one at any time. One thing the pitcher must keep in mind when throwing the half-holed ball is that it is illegal in our league for the ball to rise. This type of pitch will do little to help a player's hitting and our league is designed to help baseball hitters. Therefore throwing a rising fastball, which can be executed with the half-holed ball type, is not permitted in the game.

FIG 8-3. *Whiffle ball provides an excellent form of mental and physical practice. We've been using it as a practice form for twenty years and I'm only now starting to hear about its worth. I prefer to stage one-on-one play. This photo, featuring a two-on-two match-up, was taken at a tournament my brother Rick put together a few years back. At some points in time there were so many people in my mom's back yard that you could hear the cheers for a home run a half-mile away.*

The playing field is set up at a sixty degree as opposed to ninety degree angle. The game is played using a three-ball, two-stike at-bat — in other words, three balls you walk, two strikes you're out. The strike zone is represented by a piece of plywood 19 inches wide and 24 inches high which is mounted onto a folding chair using old baseball belts or something similar. If the ball hits the wood or the metal seat (obviously excluding the legs), it is a strike. The pitcher stands forty-eight feet away and pitching speed is not limited.

There is no base running in the whiffle ball game. Instead, runners are awarded for certain hits. For example, a ground ball past the pitcher's rubber line extended is a single. If he fields it clean before this line — you're out. With runners in double-play position, a one-handed catch on a grounder is a double play. With a man on third and a fly ball to the out-field (with less than two outs), the hitter can call tag. In this case the fielder must now throw home and hit any part of the zone structure on the fly or bounce to double him up.

A home run line is used most of the time — 80 feet down the lines and bellying out to 110 feet in straightaway center. If the ball clears the line on the fly, it is a home run. If it breaks through the line on the ground, it is a double. If the pitcher gets back and catches the ball, it is an out and if he drops the ball over the line, it's a triple.

Now, I strongly suggest that you do *not* use a whiffle ball bat — ever! To scale the timing down properly you want to use a fungo or softball bat — something having the same length and about 75 percent of your baseball bat's weight. It's all a little too quick for a real bat and this is important.

Bat Handle

Another great drill is the bat handle drill. In Figure 8-4 you can see that I'm holding a sawed-off handle of a bat. For this drill I make groups of three — a pitcher, a catcher and a hitter — in the gym or outside. Depending on the age of the players, I equip each of them with anything from a tennis ball to a real ball and a catcher's mask. I then have them pitch to each other with a live count and the hitter swinging away.

Naturally, there is no contact. The catcher does the umpiring and calls out the count loudly after each pitch. I then pick and choose which count to lock in on and watch to see how the hitter does without the bat. I watch to see if he strides on time, if he knows the strike zone areas and the counts that go with them, and if he tunnels and calculates well. I watch to see if he adjusts with two strikes. I watch his swing. It is a great way to see who is doing the mental work at the plate. After three at-bats, players rotate.

FIG 8-4. *Batting live with a sawed-off bat handle is great for tunneling and stride timing and even more effective with a catcher. It offers a great way for a coach to get the whole team practicing from the neck up.*

Beaming

Another good drill is what I call *beaming*, and it also provides a mental and physical challenge. In Figure 8-5 (a-b) you see a sheet about 15 feet away from the hitter and a dummy in the contact area. What you do here is have another player stand with a flash light to the side of the sheet while you go through your pre-swing, anticipating a certain pitch. Naturally, your friend can tell by your pre-swing what pitch your anticipating, and he has the ability to shine the flashlight behind the sheet at any time and at any location. If the right pitch illuminates at the right time and in the right place, the hitter pulls the trigger, blasting down the dummy. As you can see, the sheet has both curve ball and fastball tunneling zones. I don't recommend playing with more than two pitches

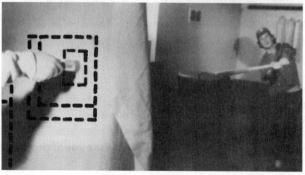

FIG 8-5 (a-b, top to bottom). *This is a drill I call "beaming." It makes use of a sheet, a flashlight, and a football dummy and keys on tunneling, guessing, and timing feel.*

because the timing on the pitcher's part to beam can be tricky, but two different speeds are easy and it's fun. You can strike each other out looking, get each other to chase bad balls; it's great practice and you can do it almost anywhere. The advantage to this drill is the fact that it keys on the hitter's tunneling and guessing, while really zeroing in on his timing feel. If the pitcher or beamer wishes to give the hitter the speed he has anticipated, he merely snaps the flashlight on just after the hitter's stride foot hits the ground. Any time the light is on before that, the pitch will be much quicker than anticipated, while the light going on after that point will make the pitch much slower. In this drill the pitcher's wind-up is imagined; however, with a third player, you can put the wind-up on the side.

If possible, use a pushbutton flashlight and block half the lens off with duct tape. When held upside down, it will show only the top of the ball on the sheet...remember under the white. Take your time putting your boxes on your sheet. Using a magic marker, walk back and forth between the sheet and the plate and dot the corners of all the different areas. Place the sheet on the floor and connect the dots. Make sure to hang the sheet at the same height daily. I didn't put the lefties curve on this sheet because I didn't want the picture to look too confusing. Also you'll find that the boxes overlap slightly. Again, I didn't put it in the picture. I also use different color markers for different pitches.

Any form of practice that combines the mental work of the hitter with the physical is a higher level of practice and more the focus of an older hitter — high school and up. A different approach must be taken when teaching a lower level hitter, a real young hitter in little league or pony league, as this is an age where the fastball is obviously the dominant pitch, and the physical simply outweighs the mental! At this age the majority of boys are better off with some good hitting drills as their prime form of practice while live hitting falls secondary. The only reason I say this is because a kid won't give a hoot about getting the good ball, walking, style or two-strike hitting until he is confident he can hit the ball hard; and at that age, that stems from a decent, well-timed swing. Also, once the kid learns to swing, the mental aspects become easier to teach because, again, he'll see the ball better.

Stride Timing

These drills that dominate a young hitter's practice are not just for the young hitter; they also keep the mature hitter physically in tune; and if you don't already know it, a swing is something that must be maintained. Sure it gets easier to maintain as you climb toward potential; however, I don't believe any hitter ever gets to the point where he outgrows his swing maintenance. What are these drills? Well, certainly, we've got to stride on time; and this comes down to simply timing different pitchers' motions. Games on TV are great; it's just the pre-swing over and over. You think fastball on one; curve on the next. You practice offsetting different weights and starting on time. You can also have a friend make-believe pitch to you. The more motions you time, the better off you'll be. Still, out of habit, when I see someone pitching, I will mentally set my stride point at a certain time in their motion.

I say stride point but *cocking point* is probably the best way to think about it. You have to time the backward flow, the cocking motion, so that you can fall forward at just the right moment. But to do this, you don't want to stop the

backward flow, or rush it. It should be smooth, just like the *"tick tock rock"* or the pendulum, back and forth, without any delay. This point is somewhere around the breaking of the pitcher's hands over his stride leg. It changes with the pitcher.

MECHANICAL

Stride Direction

The direction of the stride must be correct. Practice by drawing your heel line in the dirt, and then after striding, look down and check to see where you've landed. A gym line or piece of athletic tape on the floor will work, or even better, a straight low wall, like the picnic bench seen in Figure 8-6 or even a curbstone. By striding the heel along the wall, the hitter is forced to land his foot in the right direction.

FIG 8-6. *A picnic bench or curb stone can provide a guide for the hitter to follow the heel line.*

FIG 8-7. *Mirror work is a big help for hitters focusing on mechanics. It's like looking at a cheap video monitor.*

Mirror Work

Many of these drills can be done in front of a mirror as shown in Figure 8-7. I'm big on mirror work because you can see yourself in action. I feel as though it is valuable for hitters to check their swings from different angles and at different speeds. The ability to freeze and observe particular steps in the process can be quite helpful. Are you apart in the stretch position? Is that front foot staying put during the cocking motion? How's that front arm — pre-extending? Am I balanced in my stance? Hey, mirrors are for telling you what you look like — use them. If you don't have a full-length mirror, large store windows are great, but, keep your distance...

Hip Rotation

The best hip rotation drill may simply be concentrating on getting the legs to work together in unison. That's because when they don't work at the same time, it causes the hitter problems. The hitter lands in the stretch position and stops. Then while focusing on a full rotation, with the legs working in unison, he pops them through. After awhile, the leg movements will jell, and the hitter will feel very natural with his hip rotation. If, however, a hitter can't time these leg movements himself, I recommend moving the legs manually for him. In Figure 8-8 (a-d), you can see how I'm pushing the front knee in, while spinning the back foot. Now the hitter gets the feel of it, and most times can duplicate the movement after a short time.

FIG 8-8 (a-d, left to right). *Getting the two hips to work together smoothly can be difficult for the hitter. Here, the hitter gets the proper feel by having his hips moved manually by a spotter.*

Proper hip rotation should account for a swing where the head remains in place, or just slightly behind the starting point. You can check for this two different ways; first by lining your head up after you land with something across the plate. After you swing, you look back to that point, making sure your head and therefore body have not come too far forward. This can also be done with a rock placed on the ground in the shadow of your head. With your back to the sun and from your landing, again you swing, making sure the rock stays in your head's shadow.

There are many drills designed to help the hitter with hip rotation. Take a look a Figure 8-9 (a-b). This is a drill I call *fall backs*. Here the hitter goes through his pre-swing and swing. However, at the beginning of hip rotation, the hitter brings his back foot totally off the ground, causing him —if he's executing properly — to thrust straight back and down, where a partner catches his fall. This trains the hitter to use the front leg with power, and allows him to feel the back hip fly forward freely. It also helps the hitter to feel the slight upswing plane executed.

In Figure 8-10a the hitter has a long oar held against his lower back. The hitter is tossed whiffle balls underhand at knee level so that he can practice exploding the hips into the slight up-plane. The purpose of the oar is to isolate the movement necessary for this type of stroke.

We see this same basic concept at a more advanced level in Figure 8-10b. Here a long paddle is held up under the hitter's arms. From a stretched position and a stopped landing, the hitter calls for a toss. (The pitcher mustn't rush the hitter.) With the ball tossed high on the outside half of the zone, the hitter is forced to pull his entire swing through the zone without slack between the lower and upper halves. The result — the hitter drives the whiffle ball slightly up.

FIG 8-9 (a-b, left to right). *Above is a drill I call "fall backs" which I designed to teach hip rotation keying mainly on training the front leg for power. This drill seems to be more effective for older players as the little kids tend to horse around – allowing their partners to fall onto the ground.*

FIG 8-10 (a-b, left to right). *Both of the paddle drills pictured above are designed to get the hips moving in the slight up-plane. The low paddle (a) is more elementary while the high paddle (b) is launched from the stretch position and a more advanced maneuver.*

The Glide

The best way to practice the glide is in of an office chair. Set it as close to normal hitting height as possible, (they are usually on the low side), and sit down. Relax, have a Moxie... The whole idea here is to study the movements of the glide without having the added job of supporting the weight of your body. The office chair will support your weight as it allows for rotational and lateral movement. Stay stretched and do this one in a mirror at different angles. This can be seen in Figure 8-11.

Landing

As you now know, the landing is very important. Once you decide on your landing and you can make its moves, I would shift a little practice attention toward keeping your eyes on the same plane from the cocking motion to the landing. You can do this by putting several lines on a wall that is placed in the direction of the other batter's box. After you cock back, freeze. Then look across to see what line your eyes are closest to. After you stride you look back to see if you have stayed there. One step further, you should still be at this height through the glide and at contact. I have done this drill making soap lines on a mirror as well. Don't forget to anticipate different speed pitches during this drill.

Roped Landing

I suppose this could be a length of stride drill, but I like to think of it more as a landing drill. By taking a piece of rope and looping the two ends at the proper length, the hitter can drill with the loops of rope around his ankles and govern the length of stride and protect the quality of the landing. Remember the stride heel should not travel forward more than the length of your foot. In most cases it is more like half. This drill is seen in Figure 8-12.

Anchoring

How do you learn to anchor that front arm? After cutting a bicycle inner tube and tying one end to something stable, the hitter will take the other end in his hand, and with a bit of tension right in his stance, he will begin to slowly move through his pre-swing and swing. Naturally, as his swing rotates, the tension increases; and the hitter must fight to maintain its bent position. This setup can be seen in Figure 8-13 (a-b).

FIG 8-11. *An office chair provides a great experimentation tool for the glide. Such a chair should have the ability to rotate and move laterally.*

FIG 8-12. *A looped piece of rope tied off at the proper distance will control the stride length and enhance the landing. Also, you can still hit with this tool in place.*

 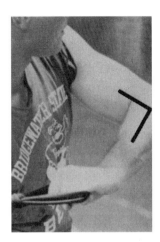

FIG 8-13 (a-b, left to right). *A bicycle inner tube cut and tied to a stationary object will allow a hitter to feel the strain placed on the front arm at the start of the swing. Be sure to begin this drill with tension.*

Another good drill for anchoring the front arm is what I call *dragging*. Here the hitter holds a rope that is attached to a weight on the ground or floor. After gaining tension in the stretch position and rope, he rotates with the strong bent front arm. This forces the hitter to maintain a strong position under a similar load but at a slower overall speed. I don't recommend that you push the arms out, you've got too much weight. Just turn the corner to that point.

Pulling a cinder block in the top of a trash can works well on the field. Figure 8-14 shows my daughter, Tamara Jolene (5) going for a ride

FIG 8-14. *Practice dragging trains the front arm to anchor while the legs and hips are overloaded. This isolates the responsibility of the body's lower half.*

on a gym cart. Dollies are good for high school and up and sitting in them will give your left-handed pitchers something to do that they can handle...

Arms and Wrists

When dealing with a young player, I like to sit him in a chair facing the pitcher. I give him a small paddle positioned properly in his hands and leveled off as he awaits the toss. I then toss him whiffle balls or tennis balls and make him focus on hitting line drives with unbroken wrists. It is important to make sure that the wrists do not roll. The paddle is a great training tool because the hitting surface diminishes when a player allows rolling wrists. This can be seen in Figure 8-15 (a-b). This drill can also be executed using a tennis racket and any of a variety of balls.

FIG 8-15 (a-b, top to bottom). *The short paddle awards unbroken wrists and proper arm execution with a large hitting surface when the swing is executed correctly.*

For an older player I do the same but he will use a real bat and I feed him dead basketballs. The dead basketballs are used for two reasons. First by providing a larger target, they allow the hitter to grow familiar with the unbroken wrist position as seen in Figure 8-16. And second, due to their weight, they train strength in both proper hand position and grip by assimilating the true impact of a baseball. For safety reasons the basketballs must be dead. This is shown in Figure 8-17. The hitter pushes the hands into the ball with a line drive as his goal.

In this drill it is suggested that the hitter tilt toward the plate from the waist before the toss. From here the hitter is assuming arm attack from the dip phase. It is fine if he straightens up after the toss for the high ball, as it is much easier to come up for a pitch than go down for one.

Driving the imaginary pitch into a rolled up rug, car tire or dummy as shown in Figure 8-18 is excellent practice as it allows the hitter to feel resistance during the swing. In fact, I believe a young hitter should never practice his swing without hitting something for resistance. The rolling wrist epidemic is too probable. This is why I view batting tees, the soft toss drill, whiffle ball or hitting tennis balls as bad practice. Any time there is minimal resistance at contact, the hitter can hit the ball more comfortably with rolling wrists. When the ball offers no resistance, kids will practice incorrectly to succeed in a drill that has little to do with hitting. It's crazy, and I see it everywhere — at all levels. Now I let kids hit whiffle balls and tennis balls but only to unbroken wrists. I don't like soft toss and the tee.

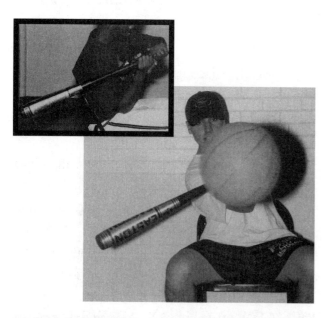

FIG 8-16 (inset) & 8-17. *Hitting the heavy weight of dead basketballs trains the hands and wrists to maintain a strong position.*

FIG 8-18. *Hitting a football dummy gives the hitter the opportunity to fully execute the swing with unbroken wrists at contact.*

JOY SPOTS

Joy Spot Bat

Ted said years ago that the bat and ball had a *joy spot* — the best spot for contact, sometimes referred to as the *sweet spot*. In Figure 8-19 the hitter is shown using a device I designed called the slide paddle. It is adjustable to any bat length and focuses on the best part of the bat to hit with. Here the hitter slides the paddle to the same distance as the joy spot on his bat. He is then peppered with whiffle balls while being forced to concentrate on this limited hitting area.

This drill helps the hitter to understand (and execute) the relationship at contact between: the joy spot on the bat, the joy spot on the ball, the proper strike zone depth and the correct degree of hip rotation in the slight up-plane. It touches on all of these areas but focuses mainly on the joy part of the bat.

Joy Spot Ball (Target Area)

I like using any ball that is bigger than a baseball for teaching target area. Examples may include a dead basketball, a nine-inch foam ball and a softball — all these or any combination of them will do the trick. In a sense, all you are doing is putting the ball and its center under a microscope for the hitter. Here the player can find the "under the white" area more obviously and approach it with solid hand position. The hitter builds an association between the barrel of the bat, under the white and a line drive. The idea is to feed the hitter the big balls and have him pepper them on a line. Then the target size can be dropped progressively keeping the same focus — line drives — with each stroke. I suggest a set of ten cuts with each different ball

FIG 8-19. *Hitting whiffle balls with a slide paddle imitates the sweet spot of the bat. The paddle portion of the tool can be adjusted to act as the joy spot for any length of bat and so is useful for teaching different age groups.*

size, finishing up with a whiffle ball or something comparable. You'll be surprised how the size of the ball will not matter when the hitter locks his focus under the white.

I would first attempt to do this in the chair as described earlier. Standing is fine, but the hitter should be facing the pitcher on the same angle as when sitting in the chair. The pitcher should slowly toss the balls underhand in such a way that they come in at the proper angle. Tossing the ball from straight on and about fifteen feet away works best. Remember, it is all right if the hitter tilts his waist in toward the plate. And don't forget this general rule of thumb — all target area drills should be practiced with the hitter using his own personal bat.

DEPTH AND ROTATION

The Trap

Maybe the best mechanical drill is hitting out of the trap. Here the hitter rehearses his longest stroke with a full body swing, tight arms and unbroken wrists. Notice in Figure 8-20 that the broomstick is held up by a highway cone and therefore can be set up on the field or in an in an open gym.

In Figure 8-21a we see a player preparing himself about arm's length away from a heavy broom stick. This stick is again held up by a cone or something similar. After the hitter gets in the stretch position he will call for the ball. Don't rush the hitter. The tosser standing about fifteen feet away will slowly toss him a dead basketball up and in. For safety, it is imperative that the ball be dead and the stick be taped spirally. The hitter now must pull his entire swing tightly through the zone exploding the arms, hands and bat into the basketball without knocking over the stick. All these balls should be pulled and the tosser should not be in any danger of being hit. Middle men should receive their tosses high and over the middle of the zone. In Figure 8-21b this middle man grounds out. The tosser will need an L screen to trap a middle man.

FIG 8-20. *Hitting out of the trap demands hip rotation with the arms in tight. The stick should be taped up in the event that it should snap.*

FIG 8-21 (a-b, top to bottom). *Hitting dead basketballs from the trap can also be effective. It is important that the balls are dead for safety reasons.*

FIG 8-22 (a-b, left to right). *Players can also trap against a wall or fence. Young players in the trap will often get in position and then want to back up. In this situation it sometimes works to place a two-by-four behind the heels of the hitter to force them in place.*

A hitter can also be trapped against a fence or wall as seen in Figure 8-22 (a-b). On an open field, high school players may hit these dead balls one hundred feet or more on a line. In a gym you can trap with whiffle balls as well. The trap with dead basketballs demands that the hips are ahead of the hands and the arms tight with proper wrist position at contact.

The trap is also great for letting the eyes and head rotate with the swing. Before contact the eyes and head will pick up the area of the field that the ball should be headed, and the ball will then jet into the hitter's view.

Another drill for getting your head out is hitting snowballs. In Figure 8-23 you can see me get out on a high outside pitch. Rather than getting a face full of snow, the hitter tends to exaggerate but it takes an exaggeration to break the habit of trying to watch the ball all the way in.

Snowballs are also good because you can use them to work the rip and even areas. Also, if the snow is wet it will stick to the bat and you can judge contact from the joy spot. For those of you who are not fortunate enough to have snow, you can wet a good size sponge and hit it on the grass.

FIG 8-23. *Hitting snowballs can be an excellent source of practice for getting the head out – that is, if you don't receive a face full of snow in return. In this photo I get out on a high and outside fastball. Note the snowball marks on the fence in the background – these can be valuable for viewing the decisions that were made in regard to the "strike zone."*

Five on Dice

This drill helps the hitter understand the depth, hip rotation degree and body position at contact of the five most critical strike zone locations. Up and in, up and away, right down the middle, low and in and low and away. It is done with three people: a feeder, a fielder and a hitter. Here the hitter sets up his hip rotation degree for one of the five locations, with his hands in tight he calls for a dead basketball and pushes it toward a fielder positioned to where it should go about ten feet away. The hitter notes his percentage of line drives in each location.

The hitter is completely rotated to the location's degree. There is no follow through and the hitter stops with unbroken wrists. It is an arm and hand drill with pre-set hip rotation! The hitter hits five balls in the same location and then the players rotate. This continues until all the locations have been completed. After the hitters complete their second round they should multiply each location total by ten to get to their line drive percentage in each location. These figures will give the coach and player a good idea of strike zone weaknesses.

The degree of hip rotation in relation to the heel line is as follows: up and in (135 degrees), low and away (45 degrees), up and away, down the middle and low and inside (90 degrees). If this drill is done correctly you'll see players squirming for balance.

Another good drill is having the hitter get to his landing and then hold a football dummy for him at different depths. By doing this you can train him to hit different locations at the proper depths. It is better if the dummy is flat on the hitting side. Then you can match the angle of the dummy to the proper angle of the bat at contact.

Pepper

Ted loved pepper and as I got older I got to understand why. It is bat, ball, depth, hips and slightly up all at unbroken wrists! I do have a few cautions with it, however. For one, I suggest that hitters play for the line drive. I mean don't play pepper for the fielder, because he'll get plenty of practice from the hitter mistakes. Play for the hitter! I also think the ball should be coming in straight on. If a wing man gets it, have him flip it to the middle. Play pepper with infielders, outfielders, and a catcher fifteen feet behind the hitter. The infield should be about twenty feet away and the outfield about forty. At this range I think all style hitters should bat from an open stance. What if there's not enough guys to run the drill? Well, in that case get in the backstop and ignore that "no peppering sign"... it's for the concession guy.

I like taping the fat part of the bat to see the early and late spots. I've seen Ted do this with a fungo. He hit pepper to me. He taped it a few inches on either side of his joy spot with white athletic tape. I used to save the tape. I would razor it off and later put it on my wall with others. I could see tendencies in this way.

I like long-distance pepper as well. For a high school player, the outfielders stand at 200 feet with the infielders in position. The hitter faces a slower batting practice pitch and hits at it with a half-speed full-rotation swing. He hits only to unbroken wrist until he grounds or flies out. In long distance pepper the hitter bats in style. The focus here is a solid swing at the proper contact, placing the ball where it should be on the field in style. In any form of pepper the hitter should work in the two-strike stroke. For every ten swings you take, two of them should be two-strike strokes.

Foam Ball Pepper

Here the hitter is facing a nine inch foam ball. It is being delivered under hand and slowly. It is coming in slightly down after its arc — the proper baseball pitch plane. The pitcher is about twenty feet away and he is delivering the ball consistently, both in terms of speed and motion. The pitcher should not alter either. He should place the ball at all strike zone locations at random. The hitter's responsibility is to step, glide, spin and push line drive after line drive to the proper field position. There are fielders to feed the pitcher and the hitter does not have to swing if the ball is out of the zone.

If the ball bounces before the fielders or goes higher than an eight-foot mark on the wall the hitter is out. The hitter hits until he grounds or pops. The hitter must swing at half speed and with unbroken wrists with the proper hip rotation for the pitch location. The ball should be hit at moderate speed so that the fielders are not flinching. Anything harder is considered out of form and the hitter is out.

This drill rehearses stride timing, the glide, target area, swing plane, hip rotation and depth. It is a great drill and also a safe one. Figure 8-24 gives you an idea of how this drill is executed.

It can also be done from the two-strike position. Here the pitcher can alter the pitch speeds slightly but not his motion. Balls that bounce once to the fielders count as a hit. With the inside-out arm position, hitters must remember to raise their target area.

FIG 8-24. *Foam ball pepper is a great drill for practicing where to hit the ball on the field. It also forces consideration toward stride timing, target area, the slight up-plane, and the glide.*

In the Cage

When you hit in a cage off a machine, you need to think about what you're doing and not about who's watching you. You need to face pitching that is equal to the average speed fastball in your league. If you are indoors, it is even better to have the pitching a little faster. Once you establish where the ball is being thrown, forget about the plate, move into the pitch for two inside pitches and then away for two outside pitches. Then make your two-strike adjustments and put one up the middle. I call this *"ins and outs with a two."* If you maintain this form you will be hitting two balls in your two-strike form for every ten pitches.

If you can adjust the speed of your machine or move to another cage for breaking ball speeds do it. Do not hit the same speed pitch all the time! Same form — ins and outs with a two.

Sometimes when dealing with younger players in the cage or on the field, I will pitch them whiffle balls hard and let them hit with a whiffle ball bat to unbroken wrists only. The extra light weight of the bat enables them to combine the feeling of unbroken wrists with timing. One of the hard parts about unbroken wrist contact is that when you miss the ball it leads to a very heavy and awkward feeling. This drill takes that away.

At times, when a young player is missing and missing, I have used a cut-off broom to help me see what is going on. If the hitter is late the baseball or machine ball will break through the top bristles of the broom, whereas if the hitter is early they will hit the bottom. The hitter must understand basic hand position at contact. Much like the paddle, if he rolls, his hitting surface will decrease dramatically. This can be seen in Figure 8-25.

FIG 8-25. *Using a cut-off broom in a live hitting situation can sometimes be useful in determining whether a hitter is swinging early or late. The bending of the bristles tells the tale.*

There are a few other odds and ends that deserve your attention, for example, slow pitching. Any time you practice against slow pitching, you're headed for both pre-extension and rolling wrists. You're better off peppering this speed. Slow pitching provides very little resistance, plus its increased arc distorts your tunneling — distorts how you see and read good pitching. Fast pitching is much better; it's pitching like you're going to see, and it's pitching that demands good mental and physical execution for success.

I don't like donuts and weighted bats either because they bend reality. When I go to the plate, I want to know the exact weight I've got to swing. I don't want to think I'm quicker than I am. I want to know exactly how quick I've got to be and exactly the weight I've got to do it with. Yeah, maybe there's a psychological advantage there because the bat feels like it's lighter, but it's not lighter, and that's what I don't like. As far as the off-season goes, weighted bats may be okay; but here we're talking about using the weights to strengthen yourself rather than to fool yourself.

While we're in the neighborhood of on-deck warm-up, I feel the on-deck hitter should not only watch the pitcher and the pitches thrown, but warm up by finding or reassuring the timing of his pre-swing, and taking "check swings." If a hitter can hit something that offers resistance, that's even better. I laugh when I see these guys whipping the bat all over the place. Stay away from that nonsense. On deck it's a short tight swing — just to an assumed contact point.

I can't say enough about hitting outside as opposed to inside because the background distances are totally different. The figure and background relationship makes these settings two different worlds. It's much harder to hit outside. Also, if you're in a cage, you lose the feedback of how hard the ball was hit, its flight and where it would have landed. Naturally, if you've got no other means, cages are great, but try to get some time outside before the season gets too close or you could be surprised.

People always ask me about machines, and I like to talk to them about them because they can be dangerous to your mechanics. Most of the machines I've seen throw consistently, but they don't allow for the hitter's pre-swing — they don't let him start his stride early — anticipate. Instead, they fire the ball out at you like it's coming out of a gun. They cause you to be late and usually lead to poor arm and hip execution from a catch-up type of swinging. I like the arm machines because you can see the arm and anticipate. Master Pitching Machine makes a great arm machine. I haven't seen a better one. Figure 8-26 is a photograph taken twelve years ago and that machine is still running great!

It's also important for the machine to be at the proper height. It's a must to have the balls coming down because again, any time the pitch

FIG 8-26. *My favorite hitting machine is the arm machine. It allows the hitter to anticipate the release of the mechanical arm.*

plane changes, your feedback will become distorted. You've got to shoot the right balls as well. If you use real baseballs or the plastic balls with stitches, the balls will move randomly; they'll tend to die, run and flutter. I don't recommend that type of practice; it's too inconsistent and it can be dangerous. Those hard dimple balls are best; they are aerodynamic, like a golf ball, and they pitch straight and consistently.

I also recommend a wooden bat when practicing because they're true. You'll feel a bad-hit ball on a wooden bat, and I think that feedback is valuable. Also, you can swing a wooden bat hundreds of times without chewing your hands to ribbons. Many aluminum bats have rubber handles, and they will wear your hands away to nothing — taped handles are even worse.

As far as batting gloves, pine tar and the whole grip-tight market, experiment with them; it really depends on where you live and you. However, if you're in the cold, I'd definitely wear batting gloves.

I highly recommend weight training as well. I've heard Ted say many times that he wishes he had done more; but I'd be careful with the upper body — with the shoulders and arms. Remember, you've got to throw the ball as well. I'd go power from the waist down, with heavy weights, at three to eight reps; and with light weight from the waist up, 15 to 20 reps. Make sure you're lifting these weights properly. A bad lift with heavy weight could cost you — be smart.

I'm also big on flexibility; good flexibility will enhance ability and decrease injury percentages. Always be sure to stretch out properly.

If you don't have access to weights, use your noggin. I mean, put your brother on your shoulders for squats and toe raises as shown in Figure 8-27, or squeeze a rubber ball as shown in Figure 8-28. Be creative. Certainly, pull-ups, push-ups and sit-ups are easy enough and bicycle tire tubes can be hooked up for a number of resistance exercises. Don't sit back — make things happen. When you do push-ups, however, I recommend you do some of them as follows. Figure 8-29 (a-b) shows something I designed called hitter's push-ups. Note how the right arm, the top arm, is close to the body; while the left arm, the bottom arm is perpendicular to the upper body. Also, notice how the power arm palm is facing ahead, while the lead arm palm is facing back. These push-ups cater more to the arm muscles involved in the swing. If you have trouble at first, I recommend that you start out doing these push-ups on your knees and then progress to your feet.

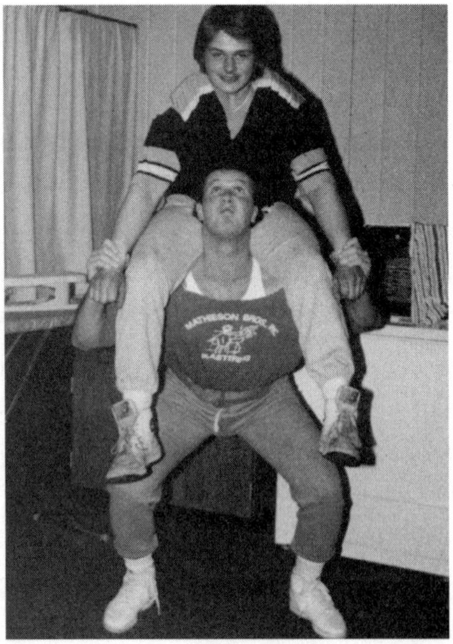

FIG 8-27. *In the above photo my brother Mark provides a "lift" in a makeshift trailor park workout.*

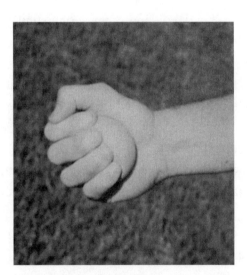

FIG 8-28. *Squeezing a rubber ball can be a good way to increase forearm strength.*

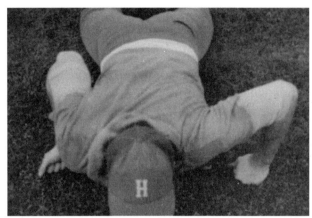

FIG 8-29 (a-b, left to right). *Here I display what I call "hitter's push-ups." These are completed with the hands in a fist and the arms positioned in the same manner that a hitter would bat.*

Finally, the attitude and philosophy surrounding the practices of any hitter are geared toward improvement. It's not recreation; it's more of a school setting — an educational setting. And just like school, practice can be the most fun you've ever had or it can be hell. Hey, if you do well, you feel great; but you try to recognize the reasons behind your success and learn. On the contrary, if you're off, you feel lousy, but you still try to recognize why and learn. Again we see the need to observe and analyze.

Now, I've talked about attitude, but a good attitude will only go as far as the motivation that fuels it. You've got to get yourself interested. You've got to use your imagination. For example, if my team was losing by 10, I would literally talk myself into the fact that we were only up by one; this kept me sharp at a time when the tendency was to simply go through the motions.

Ted spoke of motivating himself with goals — realistic goals. I think that's great; goals keep you sharp. If you happen to be down ten in the ninth and you come up with one out, sure it looks dismal, but don't pack it in for the day. Instead, say "I'm going to get a good pitch to hit because my goal is to hit .310 this year." Goals are simply another form of motivation.

There are many forms of motivation, and you know what gets you going. I wish I had a buck for every time I announced my own major league at-bat — or a friend's for that matter. Nothing was better than singing the National Anthem on the sidelines with Billy and Scott and then charging out onto the field for a hundred flies. Movies can get you all fired up. I did complete scenes from several Clint Eastwood movies. Certainly, I don't have to mention books and music. Hey, your attitude is fueled by what you see and hear, so use that to your advantage.

TROUBLESHOOTING

This short section is designed to help you find the problem. Again, the good hitter must be able to make the proper corrections and adjustments; he must have a feel for self-coaching. Here I have listed five common hitting problems and the areas where their cause is most probable:

I. Swinging late, getting jammed and popping up:

    A. Are you striding at the right time?

    B. Are you getting in the stretch position?

    C. Is the bat too heavy?

    D. Are you using your arms properly?

    E. Are you bending the back leg too much in the cocking motion for the anticipated pitch? (Offsetting too much weight)

    F. Are you losing the angle of the front foot in the cocking motion?

    G. Are you rotating the back foot?

    H. Are you just hitting the bottom of the ball as opposed to the middle?

    I. Are you launching the swing from a balanced landing?

II. Lunging:

    A. Are you keeping the back leg bent when you stride and land?

    B. Are you letting the front knee continue to bend after you land?

    C. Are you getting in the stretch position?

    D. Are you striding too far?

    E. Are you reaching that front knee out rather than landing it bent with the leg in a fixed position?

    F. Are you offsetting enough weight?

    G. Are you overloading the glide forward?

III. No power but making contact:

    A. Are you rolling your wrists?

    B. Are you getting in the stretch position?

    C. Are you launching your hips from a balanced landing?

    D. Do you have a firm grip?

    E. Is there give in the shoulders?

IV. Early, grounding out:

    A. Are you striding too early?

    B. Are you preparing well for the anticipated speed?

    C. Are you gripping the bat correctly?

    D. Is the bottom arm getting up and out of the way?

    E. Are you rolling your wrists at contact?

    F. Are you hitting the top of the ball as opposed to the middle of the ball?

    G. Are you pulling the trigger early?

V. Doing everything right and not hitting the ball as hard as often:

    A. Are you getting the good pitch to hit?

    B. Are you stealing all information possible from the pitcher?

    C. Are you making the proper changes for two-strike pitches?

    D. Are you preparing for the probable speeds correctly in the cocking motion?

    E. Did success make you lazy?

The Ted Williams League

TWL

Eighteen years ago, when teaching young hitters 8-12 years old, I noticed a few things that immediately struck me as odd. They could not use their arms the way I wanted them to and they were all late. Ninety percent of them were late — late striding and therefore late with everything else. It seemed as though their bats and arms were just too small and everything was too fast. They were much different then the older hitters I taught. I also noticed that too many of them were way off the plate and scared.

I thought about this for about two years until one day it hit me that maybe the plate was too big? Come to find out the plate that 8-12 year-old players use nationally is the same width men use in the big leagues, seventeen inches wide. But kids use shorter bats and have shorter arms. This also seemed odd. Hey, they made the distance to the mound smaller. They made the distance to the bases smaller. They made the distance to the fence smaller. They made the bats smaller. The players are smaller. Did they forget to make the plate smaller?

So now I'm out measuring arms — I mean hundreds of them! I'm at games to see what bat is most popular. How long is it? What does it weigh? I'm at sporting goods stores — "Do you sell a lot of these? How many?" I'm in every surrounding town measuring the distance between the holes in the batters box to the inside corner. Where exactly do they stand? What is the angle?

Reviewing my notes, I started to suspect that the plate and the bats being used in baseball for players ages 8-12 were out of scale. And therefore a major flaw of the game. In 1987 I started a five-year study in which I observed the same kids in two separate sets of rules. The "Regular Rules", where they used a seventeen-inch home plate and bats no longer than 31 inches, and the "Modified Rules", where they batted over a fourteen-inch home plate and had to use bats that were at least 32" and up to 36" in length. These bats were longer and thinner and slightly heavier. They were actually baseball fungo bats and girls softball bats. All bats used in the study

FIG 9-1. *A showcase group in North Hampton, Massachusetts drops the signature fourteen-inch plate for the start of a great fall program.*

FIG 9-2. *Ted Williams League MVP Billy Glynn helps me display the unjustified relationship between the length of arm and bat while holding the universal seventeen-inch home plate used for all ages. It just doesn't add up.*

were metal. All players played equal innings and the pitchers had to finish the season pitching equal innings under the guidelines of both sets of rules.

The same kids played Monday through Friday and sometimes on the weekends. And I'll tell you, when we first started, the kids wanted nothing to do with the longer bats. The bats seemed strange. Also the pitchers thought that the smaller plate was unthinkable. Some of them did not like me either, as if their dads had said I was an idiot... After about two weeks, much to my surprise, they were begging to play in the modified rules. Some were begging to use the longer bats in the regular rules! (Naturally they could not.) I was shocked.

As I thought it over, however, and it all made perfect sense. Basically here is how it went. The kids came into the study thinking the longer bats and smaller plate were stupid. The pitchers were walking everybody and the long bats were swung with pre-extended arms. Then, instinc-

tively the pitcher started to slow the ball down slightly to hit the smaller zone. The hitter in response started creeping closer to the plate. Because he was holding a longer bat the hands started coming in as well. It was almost as if his ego was teaching him how to hit. Remember at this point, due to the slightly slower pitching, the hitter has shed some fear and he is not as late with his swing. As a result, the ball starts getting hit a little more. Not hard, but more contact — more balls to be played in the infield and outfield. Then boom! A couple of the bigger kids hit long home runs because they have enough time to bring their swings into good position. Then a kid batting zero in the regular rules and maybe in his lifetime pushes one to right for a hit. Then he beats out an infield nubber in the same day. Again because of time and swing position. Then one of the older kids catches a fly ball in center going away. Now the big uncoordinated kid hits one off the fence for a single...

143

Suddenly, I found myself talking about cut-offs. With so much going on in the game the kids didn't know what to do — where to be. I noticed kids wanting to go to the outfield and I notice them in ready positions more than usual. Then it happened, the best thing of all... A nine-year-old boy came in as a reliever to face the best hitter in the study. There were a couple of runners on and it was a close game. (These games were played to win.) He threw the first pitch right down the pipe and the kid roped it foul. Then he purposely threw the second pitch much slower and almost in the dirt. The batter lunged forward, swung hard and missed. Now all the kids are watching this young pitcher and they start to get behind him. "Did you see that? He's got a change up..." On the next pitch he reached back and let one go right down the middle slightly below the letters. The hitter froze. Strike three! Good God! You'd think the Red Sox had finally won it. This little boy had taught us all a lesson! The smaller plate with smaller players needed to be pitched to no differently than the larger plate with larger players! Immediately the other pitchers started following suit. They started changing speeds and moving the ball. They started to pitch rather than just throw.

The next thing I noticed was that the bats came out to play. The hitters became much more aggressive with much more swinging in the modified game. Hitters could reach and time more balls and therefore would swing. I also noticed that very few kids were getting hit by pitches. The decreased speed of the modified rules not only kept the ball more on target but also gave hitters just enough time to avoid the stray pitch.

As these games were going on, I personally took statistics in several categories. Here are the main ones: Balls contacted fair or foul, balls pulled, balls reaching the outfield grass, strikeouts, walks, hit batsmen, balls pitched and home runs. After one hundred games the modified rules showed: Balls contacted up 8%, balls reaching the outfield grass up 40%, balls pulled up 37%, strikeouts down 17%, walks up only one per game, hit batsmen down 48%, pitched balls down 1%, and home runs up 3 to 1.

From what I had witnessed, along with these statistics, the smaller plate and longer thinner bat was clearly a better game. Now what?

I remember going down to the Little League field in my hometown and I said to one of the coaches casually, "You know, I think the plate should be smaller." I then explained why. He said, "You're crazy. The pitcher can't throw to 17 inches, never mind 14 inches. It will never happen." I later wrote a letter to Little League Baseball Incorporated and explained who I was and what I had done and asked if they would consider my findings. They said no. They felt that this had never been a problem in the past and therefore was not a problem now. At this point it was becoming obvious to me that this was not going to be easy. Many others responded the same way — almost blindly. They could not see what I was talking about. And it appeared that many didn't want to. It was all too mathematic and boring to them.

I was frustrated. I set up a meeting with Ted in Boston and I brought in the bats, the plates, the stats and I explained the whole thing. He sat and listened and asked a bunch of questions. He was more than intrigued and we discussed it for a good two and a half hours. In the next few years he became more and more interested as we continued studying it together. In 1996 we did an interview together in the Boston Globe with sportswriter Dan Shaughnessy. His article entitled "Cutting the Corners for Kid Players" explained the basic concepts of our study. In the article Ted called out for the opinion of all interested New England players and coaches. He asked if they would play by these rules and let him know what they thought. (Keep in mind, Ted is and has always been very thorough, not an easy man to convince.) The article stirred interest from as far away as Warner Robins in Georgia.

We set up a meeting in the Yawkey Pavilion at the New England Sports Museum to talk about playing by the new rules. Myself and long-time friends Charles Bradford and Bill Dawber traveled from town to town helping these small showcase-type fall programs play by the modified rules. We then returned a month to six weeks later and videotaped kids playing games along with comments from players, coaches and parents. The tapes were then forwarded directly to Ted where he viewed them at home in Hernando, Florida. About 85% of the comments were in favor of the modified rules, some of them made by coaches 15 to 40

years in the game, as well as by certified umpires, pro scouts, former college and pro players and school administrators. Ted's interest was now at its peak.

On Christmas vacation of the same year ten Boston area players and five coaches traveled to The Ted Williams Museum in Florida to play a week-long showcase against two Florida teams with Ted in attendance. The purpose of the trip was to gain Ted's final approval and offical endorsement for the Ted Williams League. The night before Ted's first scheduled appearance he fell at home and broke his hip. He was hospitalized for ten days. The games were an obvious success and again videotaped for Ted's viewing.

On January 31, 1997 Ted agreed to the formation of the Ted Williams League with its revolutionary fourteen-inch home plate and he appointed me as the league's acting commissioner. In the fall of the same year the first official season of the TWL was scheduled to play in Pembroke, Massachusetts with an opening day set for September 21st.

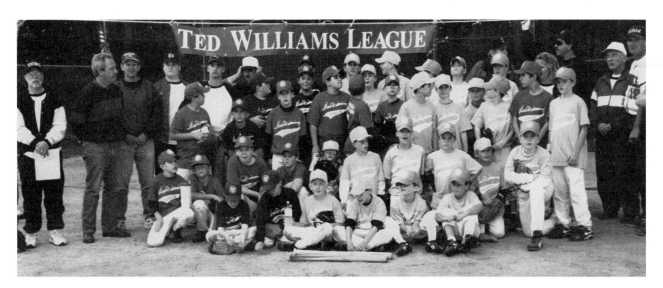

FIG 9-3. *The Ted Williams League was a great success in its first official season. The league implemented several innovative playing rules, among the most significant being an adaptation of the strike zone for players ages 8-12 years. Here, a fourteen-inch home plate replaced the old seventeen-inch plate and longer, thinner wooden bats were introduced into play.*

FIG 9-4. *Action in the new Ted Williams League was plentiful. Players got a true taste of baseball in all phases of the game.*

It was a beautiful fall afternoon and Ted, by way of a recorded phone call earlier that morning, addressed the crowd. I later threw out the first pitch to Red Sox catcher C.J. Haddad and the Ted Williams League was in swing.

After ten years of study the fourteen-inch home plate for ages 8-12 was endorsed by one of the greatest players in baseball history. At the end of official play, the Royals had defeated the Red Sox 5-1 and the Pirates beat the A's 8-7.

Through constant observation, league concepts had grown considerably beyond just a smaller home plate and the longer thinner bats studied ten years prior. By opening day, the TWL had also adopted these innovative changes: 1) the base paths moved back to 67 feet, 2) major league stealing rules were in effect, 3) a league test certification mandatory for all participating umpires and coaches, 4) slightly smaller and lighter ball used in league play, 5) a league test for motion safety and accuracy re-

quired for all pitchers before throwing in a game, 6) players do not sit out more than one inning in a row, 7) players batted in a locked order, continuous from game to game, 8) coaches allowed on the field during play, 9) any pitcher on the losing team who walks and/or hits three batters in a row is removed from the inning, 10) any pitcher considered to be a safety concern can be removed at any time, 11) all games played with a fence or home-run line.

The league operated extremely well in its first season and due to the new dimensions, things that you would normally expect to pose problems were not so bad at all. For example, take the major league stealing rules. We decided to try this for several reasons: 1) because it is part of baseball, 2) by simply increasing the distance of the base paths, the runner had further to go, 3) by making the ball not only smaller but lighter, the ball was thrown much farther and with greater control. Naturally, the kids were all for it. So we put it in.

It ended up that our biggest challenge was the pitcher understanding the stretch and the balk; within a week, however, they had it down. I believe we had only four blatant balks the entire season. Remember, all the coaches must be certified and therefore the proper instruction was readily available. As far as the runners go, the timing was fine. Many of the runners were safe due to dropped balls and poor middle infield positioning. We had one playoff game where five kids tried to steal second and three were thrown out. That should give you an idea. I feel that the base paths were another poorly calculated dimension. It appears that the customary sixty-foot length led youth baseball to hold the runner to the base because the catcher could not throw anyone out otherwise. That is not the case in the TWL.

There were a lot of pleasant surprises that came along with the leagues changes. For example, by the pitcher having a live runner and the runner having a lead, the runners learned about the jeopardy of being off the bag and the pitcher and catcher built that visual relationship with the baseman. The leading runner seemed to bring an education with him.

The catching position was more popular than usual. The catcher in the TWL was — the catcher! Plays at the plate, blocking in the dirt, communication, runners going and calling different speed pitches. They did a great job.

Certainly another example was the wooden bat. We did not force its use but permitted specially designed wooden bats that looked similar to fungo bats, the longest being a 34". Four teams played a nine-game schedule with playoffs and due to the new combined forces of pitch speed, ball weight and bat speed — not one of them broke! Not a single one! And there were several long home runs hit with them.

I talked about the bases being moved back to allow for base stealing, but what about the rest of the game? I got more compliments about this than anything! In the TWL if you hit a hard ground ball to third and the third baseman blocks it, he just picks it up and throws you out. If you hit a ball in the third base/shortstop hole and the shortstop fields it clean, unless you're real fast, you're out. If the second baseman dives and stops a ball — you're out. Due to the base path distances under the regular rules, these players are most often safe. Take this example — man on second, clean single to the outfield, runner trying to score. That runner must now run fourteen extra feet. What's the outcome? Outfielders started to get hungry and cutoff men gained an extra motivation for being in the proper position.

FIG 9-5. *The TWL allows the use of bats that are slightly longer and thinner than what has customarily been used in youth baseball. These bats are encouraged because they can cover the fourteen-inch plate effectively when using the proper hitting mechanics.*

Having coaches on the field is one of my favorite changes. Why have a coach on the bench with three players when there are nine on the diamond? It is designed to keep coaching at a speaking level rather than having it constantly at a shouting level. Most of the coaches wandered behind the infielders on the outfield grass, therefore enabling them to coach the outfield and the infield. "Hey, Bobby you're bag right?" "Joe, move over this way a little more — he's a lefty." "Alex, let us know if he goes." I wandered the field as the commissioner of the league every game of the season. I bet I made a couple of hundred coaching comments, but the parents didn't hear them, the fans didn't hear them, only the players did. And we think that's how it should be.

FIG 9-6 & 9-7 (inset). *Coaching on and off the field – the TWL allows for coaches to walk the playing field while the action is going on. TWL Red Sox coach Warren Place takes position between the infield and outfield in 9-6. From this position he can comment quickly and quietly to all fielders. Meanwhile, in 9-7 I escort a team off the field following league action.*

Without going on and on, I want to list the things I saw happen in the Ted Williams League which I feel are beneficial to baseball. If you're into youth baseball, you'll know what I mean:

1) it was a better scaled-down version of the game

2) the hitters were more offensive than defensive

3) the pitcher had to learn to pitch rather than just throw

4) successful pitchers were not just big strong kids with live arms

5) more all-around action

6) easier to teach the game with the ball in play more often

7) the catcher was not just a backstop and did not have to constantly deal with an overthrowing pitcher

8) easier game on the plate umpire, more enjoyable for the base umpire

9) more outfield interest

10) more plays at second, third and home

11) a legitimate chance at a various double plays

12) the fielder was further back and had more time to play the ball

13) it hosted a wider span of talent

14) the less skilled players could survive and learn

15) a higher level of challenges for all players

16) there was a TWL "Nolan Ryan," but there was only one (not one on each team)

17) the hitter could reach bad pitches and would swing

18) the coach could provide more information because there were more chances to do so (more learning moments)

19) it was more fun for everybody

FIG 9-8. *Arthur "Buzz" Hamon (pictured on right), the director of the Ted Williams Museum and Hitters Hall of Fame in Hernando, Florida, hosted Ted's personal TWL showcase on the museum grounds. An enthusiastic supporter of TWL efforts, Buzz was out there everyday cheering the kids on, talking with parents, and leading groups on museum tours.*

Now think about hitting? You can see why hitters pre-extend! Especially the small hitters. You can see why they are late! You can see why they are afraid! They often start out that way at eight years old, thousands and thousands of them and it's been going on for over fifty years. Kids are playing in a game where the advantage and disadvantage between the pitcher and hitter is dramatically off balance due to an oversized home plate. The little pitcher has an advantage of strike zone width that he does not deserve and the little hitter cannot possibly defend against it to potential. Naturally, the little pitcher finds most of his success with velocity, and this velocity, which was originally invited into his game by an oversight, complicates matters more by scaring the hitter further away from the plate.

What is perhaps most important about the Ted Williams League is that it provides a true scaled-down version of the actual game. We did not change the game to make it easier for the hitter or harder for the pitcher. We adjusted the game to where it should have been from the start. After ten years of looking at it — and looking at it — I am convinced that between the ages of 8-12 years old I did not play baseball at all! I merely played an out-of-scale version of a similar, but less enjoyable game. Are you playing baseball? Are you coaching baseball?

Am I putting down any league or their efforts? Absolutely not! If you are out there for kids, then I'm with you! I'm just trying to make everyone's time a little better spent. I think baseball is the greatest of games — a dress rehearsal for life. But many kids drop out at the worst time of all — right about age thirteen. Boy, if

there was ever a time to have a kid out there it's thirteen. Why do they quit? Because from 8-12 years old — it's boring. At thirteen or fourteen, when a kid starts making more decisions on his own, he starts thinking about what baseball really meant to him. In most cases it doesn't mean enough for him to continue.

It is the intention of the Ted Williams League to eventually host players six years old to retirement. We started in the 8-12 year age bracket for all the reasons previously mentioned. We are hoping to run our first teen-age league late in the summer of 1998.

FIG 9-9. *Last fall in its first official season the Ted Williams League played four teams between the ages of 8-12. This fall the league is expected to triple in size while operating in several other areas as well.*

FIG 9-10. *The pennant above listed all the participants in the "First Official Season" of the Ted Williams League.*

Participants in the first official season of the Ted Williams League were as follows:

Red Sox players: Greg Banks, Sam Bargar, Mike Barra, Kevin Denien, John Fox, Brian Haddad, C.J. Haddad, Daniel O'Reilly, Sean O'Reilly, Brad Royer, Jimmy Taddai, and Joseph Varao.

Coaches: Warren Place and Mark Kenerson.

Royals players: Tony Bagni, Eddie Crowell, Wolfgang Dawson, Billy Glynn, Marcus Glynn, Brendan Laffin, Bill Lambert, Matthew Lombard, Mike MacDonald, Derrick Wedge, Devon Wedge, Anthony Valanzola.

Coach: Greg Davis.

A's players: Nicholas Cunningham, Brian Dorney, Greg Fell, Ryan Garrity, Benjamin Green, Sean Kenney, Mark Kowaleski, Thomas Lewek, Andy MacDonald, Daniel Rattigan, Matthew Sherman, Nathan Weber.

Coaches: Les Weber and Dave Lewek.

Pirates players: Lachlan Burgess, Justin Boyd, Jay Costa, Erik Dana, Paul Davis, Dale Esker, Joshua Glynn, Peter Koury, Ryan Landis, Matt Lincoln, Gary Patten, Brian Rooney.

Coach: Paul Rooney.

Special thanks to the following for their participation and contributions:

Announcer: Bill Dawber

Scorers: Bob Sherman and Terri Butler

Clinician: Coach Fred Brown

Umpires: Charles Bradford, Dave Bonnell and Brian Butler

Concession stand attendants: Kathryn Butler and Stephanie McKenney.

Ted Williams League

Please send me additional Information about starting a Ted Williams Chapter in my area.

Name_____

Address_____

City or town_____

State_____**Zip**_____

Fax Number_____

Telephone_____

Months of the year you would be playing?_____

Age of players you are interested in playing?_____

Do you need this information in another language?_____

Mail to: The Ted Williams League, P.O. Box 1127, Pembroke, MA 02359
Or call: 1 (800) 895-8925

P.O. Box 1127, Pembroke, MA 02359
1-800-895-8925

FIG 9-11. *Above is an inquiry form designed for this book. If you fill out this form (or a copy) and mail it to the Ted Williams League office, you will receive instructions and guidelines for starting a TWL in your area.*

HIT YOUR POTENTIAL — HITTER'S QUIZ

1) The slight upswing is a power hitter's stroke. _____

2) Style allows a hitter to do anything he wants. _____

3) Rolling wrists will bring contact to the top of the ball. _____

4) The two-strike stroke requires the hitter to get under the white. _____

5) The stretch position locks the lower body to the upper. _____

6) Timing is adjusted by altering the stride's starting time. _____

7) The arms and hands travel in a circular path. _____

8) The bottom arm provides most of the power in the swing. _____

9) Hitters will bat in the "rip area" most of the time. _____

10) The stride should be fifteen inches long. _____

11) The inside high pitch requires the most movement to hit. _____

12) When the count is 2-0, we are always looking for the fastball. _____

13) The singles hitter should be the best two-strike hitter. _____

14) Always take the first pitch. _____

15) The top of the ball appears brighter than the bottom. _____

16) The back knee controls the offsetting of weight. _____

17) Slow batting practice is a great confidence booster. _____

18) The most popular hitting style is that of the middle man. _____

19) Good hitters can see the ball hit the bat. _____

20) Once your swing is in place you'll never lose it. _____

(Answers found on page 154)

FIG 9-12. *Umpire Charles Bradford gets ready for TWL action. Charlie has been a faithful pioneer of the league for over ten years and has come to be known as "Uncle Charlie." Many of the photos in this book as well as in* **Disciple of a Master** *were taken by Charlie. Below you will find the umpire's ruling on the quiz questions from the previous page.*

HIT YOUR POTENTIAL — HITTER'S QUIZ

Answers:

1)	False	6)	False	11)	True	16)	True
2)	False	7)	False	12)	False	17)	False
3)	True	8)	False	13)	True	18)	True
4)	False	9)	False	14)	False	19)	False
5)	True	10)	False	15)	True	20)	False

A Few Anticipated Questions

PINCH HITTING

This section highlights the answers to a few questions that I feel you may be inclined to ask; for example, how can you take a pitch you haven't seen if you're pinch-hitting or when they change pitchers on you in the fifth? This is a good question because many times these situations are tight situations, and I agree that often you cannot afford to take a pitch for information purposes. So what do you do? Well, the answer really depends on what you have done in the past; again, not just on that day, but in previous meetings. Regardless of whether you're in the game or not, the good hitter will be doing his homework and remember his past assignments. When you've done your homework, weighing and measuring the situation at

FIG 10-1. *Pinch hitting is very difficult and it is crucial that a pinch hitter know the game situation. If possible, the hitter should be aware of past experiences with the pitcher he is about to face.*

hand will be much easier, and the observant hitter will have no problem formulating his idea of a good ball for this type of an at-bat. Again, it all comes down to how you're going to play the at-bat; and naturally, the more alert you've been, the more accurate your decision will be. Depending upon the pitcher's talent, you may decide to take a peek at one; or on the other hand, you may decide to go after the first ball if it meets your requirements. If you've never faced the pitcher before (depending upon the game situation), you might want to use your two-strike swing throughout the entire at-bat.

The bottom line is information; and a good hitter steals and remembers every piece of information in sight. Whether he is pinch-hitting or facing a reliever, the good hitter will always have an information edge.

CONTROLLED HEADSTART

There are also a couple of points in reference to stride. First off, I said stride was a controlled headstart, and I want to expand on that because often hitters don't understand that the stride is only a part of the swing. Just because a hitter strides on time and glides, he shouldn't feel obligated to swing. What makes the stride a controlled headstart is the fact that only the legs can start the swing — the rotation of the hips. The stride and the swing are really two separate pieces of the puzzle. It's a stride and then a decision to swing that "looks like" one smooth motion.

Also, you should note that both guessing and good timing technique will eliminate a hitter's fear of striding on time and build confidence. Learning the tie between guessing, calculating, and timing is a great day for any hitter because he'll experience the consistent advantage of being on time for every anticipated pitch. After this experience, the hitter usually finds himself despising any late strides while his confidence starts saying things like, *"I can hit that now."* Proper use of guessing and timing can bring a hitter a long way in a short time.

STRIDE OFF MOTION

Often after hearing my spiel on timing, someone will question; "Why not forget about bending the back leg for different offsettings of weight and fluctuate the balance point by starting the stride at different points of the pitcher's delivery?" Why not? Just take a look at Figure 10-2. Well, although it may sound like a logical idea, it's impossible because the pitcher's arm is traveling much too fast for you to see and remember different starting times. These people are talking about three different speed pitches, all having different starting times, recognized by watching an object moving fast, 60 feet away. The speed of the pitcher's arm plus the angle in which you would be trying to identify these starting times makes this idea impossible — the hand is quicker than the eye.

What I want you to realize is that this task can only be accomplished by feeling the different weight shifts and starting at a time in the pitcher's motion that can be easily recognized, which is before the high-speed extension from the throwing arm's elbow joint.

Unfortunately, now and then you will face somebody who is way out of the average timing spectrum of your league; I mean if your league's average fastball is 80 with the curve around 65. On a given night you may face someone throwing a 65-mile-an-hour fastball and a 50-mile-an-hour curve. It is almost as if you cannot swing the pendulum back far enough...

FIG 10-2. *Some people believe that the stride should start at different points in the pitcher's motion for different velocities – I disagree. The stride should start before the high-speed extension of the pitcher's elbow joint.*

On these nights I would treat that pitcher differently and set my stride later in his motion — at the release point. Now keep in mind this may only happen two times in a season. This pitcher in an odd way can be very destructive to a hitter. If he gets you out he can really spin you mentally. Any pitcher that beats you on the early side of timing cuts you deep. Treat him with respect and stride later in his motion.

DRAWING A LINE

This reminds me of something else I want to say. Throughout this book I have tried very hard to speak in simple terms about something very complex. Hitting is not an easy subject to talk or write about. It reminds me of algebra, everything building and depending on its previous steps. What I'm getting at is that a few times I have skipped a detailed explanation and presented the concept in a way that I felt it could be easily understood and experienced.

FIG 10-3. *Some hitters move a little in their stance which is fine. I think this is a way of dealing with tension. It should not, however, disrupt the pendulum timing in any way.*

RHYTHM

What about movement in the stance — rhythm? Lau called it an "absolute," claiming that all hitters move a bit in the box. Whether it's a flapping Joe Morgan elbow or a wagging Carl Yaztremski bat, good hitters move while they wait. I view rhythm as a way of dealing with tension and not a mechanic. Mechanically speaking, your pre-swing will provide all the preliminary movement you need to swing. You don't have to move before the cocking motion unless you feel a need to.

HITTING TO ALL FIELDS

We've all heard about hitting to all fields. It is something that young hitters strive for and dads brag about. Stay away from it! Bottom line, it increases your strike zone. Not in the two-dimensional sense of width and height, but rather in its depth. Your strike zone becomes much deeper. It becomes filled with more balls to hit — to time! Too much to remember — too much to practice! And where is the return on

it? Your dad bragging? "Oh, he hits to all fields — he just goes with the pitch." Yeah. What's his average? I asked Ted about it fifteen years ago and he quickly said: "Hard!" We then talked about strike-zone depth. Hey, we all drop one the other way at times, but unless we've been asked to do so, it is a mistake, not an intention.

THE FEET

The movements of the feet are important in hitting because they tell a balance story. The front foot should roll over and the back should pivot and even flop over itself on the up-and-in pitch. The greater the hip rotation the more the rolling and flopping. Now much of the rolling and flopping occurs just after contact depending on the pitch's location. However, if this is not happening you are cutting your hip rotation short. Players who struggle moving their feet usually are not balanced at the start of the swing. Many times they did not create the stretch position either. To see these points further illustrated, take a look at Figures 10-4 (a-c) and 10-5 (a-c).

MOVING THE AREAS

What if you have a high rip area as I do and the pitcher convinces you that he's going to keep it at the knees all day long? Should you take two low strikes? No. In this case I would move my feet further apart, bend my knees more and mentally lower the rip and even areas. By doing this, again, we have favored timing over location. A hitter can hit an anticipated pitch in a tough area much better than he can hit whatever comes with two strikes. Remember, with two strikes, guessing, our number one timing resource, has been sacrificed.

FIG 10-4 (a-c, left to right). *As the front leg extends, the front heel swings under, and the foot then rolls over with the follow through.*

FIG 10-5 (a-c, left to right). With the weight favoring the little toe side of the foot in the follow through, back foot rotation should occur on the ball of the foot.

On the contrary, what if you've got a low rip area and a pitcher proves to be consistently upstairs? Do the opposite. Raise your rip and even areas, but please understand that in both of these cases I'm talking about a pitcher you know. This isn't a decision you want to make after three batters so don't get carried away with this. Use it only against pitchers who demand its use.

ANOTHER .400 HITTER

Do I think there will be another .400 hitter? You bet there will be; he's way behind schedule. He needs only to be a little smarter, to take a more concentrated look at style and learn the two-strike stroke. It could happen anytime — provided the game stays the same! If they raise the mound or make some other change then I make no promises.

FRONT FOOT ANGLE

Earlier I talked about how the front-foot toe should not "turn back" with the front knee in the cocking motion. While I felt it would be confusing to expound at that point, now I feel you can fully understand that if the front leg swings too far back it will delay the batter from reaching the stretch position at the proper time, causing his bat to be late. Figure 10-6 displays this position.

FIG 10-6. *Here is an example of a front foot that has rotated back with the front knee. This will lead to a lagging swing.*

I DON'T GUESS

Sometimes I'm asked about the good hitters who claim in the media that they don't guess at the plate. I usually answer by asking, "Who controls a hitter's salary?" When most answer the club owner, I disagree. The people who pay a hitter are the people who pitch to him. Therefore I would call you naive if you think a guy making three million dollars a year is going to tell *Sports Illustrated* and every pitcher in his league that he guesses. The obvious thing to do is to claim you do not. If pitchers are stupid enough to believe that, then they'll really think you're good and as a result challenge you more often with their best pitch. This in turn makes guessing much easier.

TOO HARD NOW

Due to the player's comfort and confidence with his past approach, I know many coaches may feel that applying this theory at the professional, college or high school level may be too difficult. With the pressure and learning environments of these levels in mind I can't argue that point. But I have a friend from high school — Greg Davis — who made a complete change at 28 years old and did a nice job with it. Old dogs can learn new tricks.

While I am more than confident that good instruction can improve hitters at any level, realistically I know good instruction will not be present most of the time.

FOLLOW THROUGH

Everybody talks about the follow through, and to avoid being too much of a radical, I've included an example of the proper technique in Figure 10-7. Notice how the body has completely rotated with the feet flopped over. If you do everything right before this phase, chances are your follow through will be camera ready.

What about the Charlie Lau theory — let-go-of-the-bat follow through? Because the Lau theory brings the hitter's weight onto the front leg with a planted and closed front foot, the hitter runs out of hip rotation early. This, for comfort's sake, forces the hitter to let go of the bat with the top arm as shown in Figure 10-8 (the batter's right arm cannot reach the point where the body would naturally bring the bat). Not only do I think this is foolishness, I also think these hitters look like they should be playing in the woods with Christopher Robin to the tune of a flute player dressed happily in tights with a belled cap.

LIGHT BATS

You've probably been thinking that Ted Williams was a great supporter of light bats, and that what I'm saying goes against his views. Well first off, I think Ted was a strong advocate of the hitter choosing the correct bat, and that's important. Ted's view was that you should use the lightest bat that can do the job, and I agree with this view. But remember, outside pitches are part of the job, too. If you asked me, "Did Ted Williams use a light bat," my answer would be, "No." The way I see it, for his ability, "The Splendid Splinter" used a good bat, a smart bat. Hey, most of the home-run hitters around Ted's era were more compact than he and the bats they used would have seemed heavy by comparison. But to say that Ted used a "light" bat wouldn't really be accurate, as "light" can really only be defined according to your ability and mechanical execution. In fact, the section on bats in *The Science of Hitting* is entitled, "Light but right."

I had the privilege of spending a day talking hitting with one of Ted's former players, Mike Epstien, a real serious hitting coach and a great guy. When Mike was heading home to California, my buddy Greg gave Mike this huge wooden bat as a momento of his trip to Boston. It was 37 and a half inches long and weighed about 35 to 36 ounces. I had been experimenting with it for about a year. Ted picked it up one day and said, "Boy, I guess this is an experiment..." Mike was at the time coaching minor leaguers and in pursuit of a big-league managing postion. We were in close contact during this time period and one day he says to me, "I got this monster minor-leaguer who has hit 15 home runs in about a month."

"Wow," I said.

FIG 10-7. *The hitter's follow through should favor the back leg with the feet moving freely.*

FIG 10-8. *In this example of poor technique, the hitter is forward over his front foot which causes the front foot and leg to be restricted.*

Then he told me that he had hit them with the bat Greg had given him! I almost fell off my chair. What is light? What is right? It depends on you.

CROSS COACHING

What if you start making progress with this theory and your coach crosses you up? That is, he wants you to swing down. Well, there are two main characteristics I've found in most coaches; 1) they all have egos, and 2) they all love to win. What this boils down to is that if you advertise the fact that you're taking pride in a new hitting approach other than what they have shown you, they may be offended and they will surely make note of it. Sure enough, with the first sign of failure — you'll hear about it.

On the other hand, the tendency is to leave well enough alone; therefore, if you're doing well with whatever you're doing you'll prob-

ably be in the clear. If your coach is closed-minded, I advise keeping a very low profile. However, if your coach is sincerely open-minded, tell him what you're trying to do and why. You may be putting a state championship in his ear.

MOMENTUM

Sometimes, when I talk about the two-strike position, someone will argue that a 225-lb. Steve Ferroli can use this shortened stroke and still have the power to hit the ball with authority; however, the 150-lb. shortstop can't get the ball past the pitcher with that stroke. Well, when coaches use the word power in hitting they really mean "momentum" (a mass times a velocity) and what I want hitters to understand is that many times that 150-lb. shortstop has the ability to generate every bit as much momentum or power as the 200-lb. hitter. What I'm saying is that if the quick fast running short stop is swinging his 150 lb. at 100 m.p.h. while the 200 lb. hitter is swinging his weight at 75 m.p.h. they have created an equal amount of momentum. What happens today is that the quick light hitters get lured away from using their bodies at an early age. They're taught to use their arms to hit and their legs to run, when they should be using their legs to hit and then their legs again to run. Obviously, this applies to all swings, not just the two-strike swing.

I played with or against many smaller guys who used their bodies well and hit the ball real hard for their size — Adam Frattazio, Mike Pazzanese, Tom Reardon and Ray Bresnahan to name a few. Brady Anderson would be a good major-league example. I read once where Rod Carew said he could hit balls 400 feet but for style sake chose not to.

FIG 10-9. *In my summer camp, coaches who don't adhere to logic are shown the door.*

CHEATING STYLE

Sometimes I see hitters who cop out on their true style. They have the ability to hit .330 with 30 home runs but they choose to push the ball the other way for their entire career. They use the inside-out stroke all the time. I think of these players as businessmen rather than hitters. It's a long way from Ted Williams and how I see sport. Is there a style of hitting that emphasizes pushing the ball the other way all the time? Boring! To me that's like saying, "I can't!" If this hitting style exists, it is for a struggler and certainly not a star.

FIGURED OUT

Often, someone will ask what if the pitchers know the areas you like and keep their pitches away from them; should you take two strikes? No. That's when it gets to be fun because now you can look for location as well. Hey, they used to pitch Ted away with sliders, a location and pitch he didn't care for, and he had a field day with it because any time you can predict both the pitch and location your timing should be next to perfect. What could be more fun?

EVEN STANCE FOR KIDS

I said earlier that the majority of hitters follow the middle man style of hitting and it's true, but when teaching a young boy (ages 8-12) I always make it a point to set them up as pull hitters. I do this because the straight stride aids them in clearing the hips. They'll have plenty of time to adjust when they get older and have a better understanding of how the strike zone is approached.

HEAD MOVES BACK

Some people ask me if I think the head moves back during the swing. I think it does. You can see this in Figure 10-10 (a-b). Sometimes I'm questioned whether this affects what I see. No. Again, after a swing decision, my eyes are starting toward the field of the anticipated hit. You know with the head coming back I feel I gain time. It's like going away for a football pass as opposed to coming in for one.

FIG 10-10 (a-b, top to bottom). *From a marked starting point, here we see the difference in head movement between the Lau and Williams theory from a different angle.*

EARLY STRETCH

Sometimes, I'm asked why not just start in the stretch position? Sparing the details, you'll be quicker if you put the to-be-used muscles on stretch just an instant before the task. It has to do with an elastic-type characteristic of muscle fiber. Also, the position is very uncomfortable to maintain for all that time.

3 AND 1

Many times I'm asked about the 3 and 1 count. If you have prepared for a fastball in the rip area and you get a fastball for a strike — something out of that area — should you swing or should you take it and go 3-and-2? Well, it depends on the pitcher and the game situation. If the pitcher's tough, you might want to extend to the even area at 3-and-1. On the other hand, if he's "cake" stay in the rip area and go to 3-and-2. If you need the long ball, and you're the man to do it, take a shot at the 3-and-1 pitch if it's not in a bad spot. Remember, to hit consistently with two strikes, you've got to sacrifice power.

TOO WEAK

What if a kid isn't strong enough to swing the proper bat? Well, that's easy — he then works at getting strong enough so he can! We don't want to make a technical adjustment in this case, I mean we shouldn't say okay, use a light bat and reach. This kid is no different than the kid who can't dribble left-handed — he's got to do the work to get there. In the meantime, without broadcasting it, he'll just have to sacrifice the outside corner using something he can handle correctly.

THINKING IN DETAIL

Do you know what I like about hitting the most? The fact that it forces you to think in detail. What part of the ball? What part of the bat? How many ounces? How fast? Something feels funny, what is it? What was that pitch? Are you sure? Who is warming up? What's he got? What kind of a day is it? The problem with a young hitter is that most cannot comprehend the importance of detail. They have not lived long enough. Most will work hard but you have to stay on them for consistency.

GOOF-UPS

You may have noticed that I took some of these pictures with the label facing up and yes, in some photos the ball is hanging on a string. You should have seen my friend Kenny holding the fishing rod... I hope you're this observant in a game.

FIG 10-11. *Many of my players over the years have come to study the game as I have. They have learned to watch and store information. They have learned to be patient, to practice. I learned these same things from Ted and I'm glad to pass them along to the next generation of hitters.*

YOUR KIDS

I often run into dads, moms, coaches or league officials who are trying to do the best for their kids. My advice here is to buy all our information. We have video tapes as well as this book and other instructional ideas planned as well. Am I trying to sell you something? Yes. Let's say it costs you one hundred dollars total for the information. I've seen dozens of dads pay a hundred dollars for the wrong bat... Get the information. If you're looking for hands-on instruction perhaps the player could attend one of our camps. Or maybe you could investigate bringing one of our camps to you. We do all sorts of programs and anything is possible. We have had small businesses or leagues sponsor a program in a town. We've had dads organize them by renting gyms and running ads on their own. We can tailor them to your needs. Here is my favorite. I come out there on a Friday morning. Friday night we run a coaching clinic, lectures, drills, tests — everything. At the end of the coaches' clinic we give assignments to various coaches, then on Saturday and maybe Sunday as well your coaches run a clinic for your kids under my direction. It is a fun weekend with loads of results.

You can reach the Ted Williams League at:

Toll free – (800) 895-8925

Address – **The Ted Williams League**
P.O. Box 1127
Pembroke, MA 02359

Website – **www.hitter.com**

FIG 10-12. *Above I am shown running a full baseball clinic for a group of thirteen and fourteen-year-olds in Omaha, Nebraska. Such clinics are a great opportunity to provide local coaches across the country with a ton of useful information.*

FIG 10-13. *These two Boston area boys along with eight others traveled all the way to Florida to participate in the Ted Williams League Museum Showcase. Here the boys sign the signature fourteen-inch home plate and newly designed TWL bat to be presented to Ted Williams. These boys certainly exemplify players with a love for the game.*

A DAY IN THE LIFE

I was doing a clinic one day in Boston and I was watching a kid take some cuts in the cage. I heard a voice behind me, "You're going to quiet those feet aren't you?" I didn't even bother to turn around. Then the voice called out again, "Don't you think he's opening up too soon?" Finally, after about the fifth comment and as the hitters were switching positions in the cage, I turn around to see this good looking man about forty-five years old coming toward me with his hand out.

"Hi, I'm..." he says his name.

I recognized the name immediately and the man now looked familiar as well. He was a former big-leaguer who had played fifteen years or so at the professional level. Incidentally, this man was also an avid follower of the Lau approach to hitting.

He told me what a "great setup" we had and went on and on and I thanked him. He had heard of me and spoke highly of Ted Williams and this was nice. Then he said that someone like me should be in... well, let's just say he said he knew a lot of people and claimed he might be able to land me a coaching job. (I was still impressed by things like that back then and so he had my interest, so to speak.) The former big-leaguer then offered to return the next day and guest speak to the kids for free, which I took him up on. After all, the kids eat that pro stuff up and it happens to be one detail that I cannot offer them...

The next day he returned and gave a great lecture on how fortunate the youth in America are to have the opportunity to grow up playing baseball. He gave the kids a sense of just how lucky they were in comparison to some of the situations they could be in. The talk was well prepared and I admit I was impressed, pleased to see the kids getting something out of it.

At the end of the lecture, however, he went on to say, "Unfortunately there is one thing that Steve Ferroli cannot teach you and that is the confident composure of a professional baseball player. I would like to demonstrate that for you." At this point I was a little hurt but they didn't raise puppies in my house and so I thought to myself, "Okay, maybe this guy's got a point." I let the comment go without a reaction and awaited the demonstration that he had in store for the kids. He then continued, "To prove this to you I would like to challenge Steve to a hitting contest. You kids pick the winner and the loser buys the entire camp pizza tomorrow for lunch!" Well, let me tell you the kids were on fire! Yeah! Yeah!

"Are we on, Steve?" he asked.

"I guess so," I replied.

I let my guest pick the speed (about seventy-five he chose) and I let him warm up. This guy truly swung the bat right out of Charlie Lau's book and without question he did have the poise of a professional — he wasn't nervous at all. He asked me if I wanted to take a few swings and I declined. Then he said, "Okay, I'll hit first," but before he did so he looked at my buddy Charlie and went on, "he's in trouble now." This is when Charlie replied, "You're the one in trouble."

The man stepped up, hit the ball, and hit it well — line drives and hard grounders. When I stepped in there was near dead silence. The kids were afraid for me, you know because they like me. What they didn't know and what this former big-leaguer didn't know was that I had given my life to hitting — my life!

So what happened on the first pitch? I took it! Then I began laying them out, rope after rope. I purposely backed away from the plate for about five cuts to drill them off the machine. My guest could hear the contact loud and clear. Blam! Blam! Blam!

When it was over the kids were clapping and chanting for me. My opponent, with his eyes watered up, said nice job and wandered off into the outfield for some time to himself. Not long after, I got my kids into a game with the other coaches and jogged out to the man. He would not look me in the eye. I thanked him for talking to my kids and said that I'd buy the pizza. Then I jogged away. The next time I looked up, our visitor was gone.

It's important to understand that just because a player isn't burning up the major leagues doesn't mean he can't hit and improve his hitting. In my case I simply wasn't ready early enough. Through the eyes of approach, I think that hitting is an older player's skill. I think most players become much better hitters in later years — not quicker, stronger or more powerful but technically more sound. I think Ted Williams was much better executing as an older player. I, too, am a much better hitter than I was in this story.

I guess it's pretty simple — I want you to know that I can hit. I mean, that's the bottom line isn't it? This book, like *The Science of Hitting*, was also written by a hitter. Could I hit in the big leagues today? Yes. In fact, I believe I would do very well. Is this what I want to do? No. Coaching is what is important to me now, developing the Ted Williams League and helping countless youngsters become better hitters, better ball players, better people.

A LOVE FOR THE GAME

What I would like to see in the future is more players who show a true love for the game. I know the players who really love it — they're the ones who practice it and practice it, the ones who can't get enough of it. When I think of this love or dedication for the game of baseball, a couple of names come to my mind immediately. Darrell Bucky Brandon for one. Here was a guy who *loved* baseball. He played in the big leagues for years, and I had the pleasure to get to know him when he was released. He would call me up and pitch to me or I would catch him. We played together in local leagues and he was very good to me — just a regular guy willing to talk baseball all day long.

Another person who comes to mind is Jack Mountain. Jack played triple-A ball for years and I guess at one point he was said to have the best arm in the Boston Red Sox farm system. He was an outfielder with a sweet left-handed stroke, and a player who stepped on the field with a great attitude every day. I know that I learned a lot from him during the time we played together.

Another name worth metioning is that of Junior Rentas, a Boston Park League hitting legend. I don't even know Junior personally but I've seen him play and at forty-two or so years old it is evident that this guy still loves the game.

I've had college players travel across the country to learn how to hit and I've loved to teach every one of them: Russ Hubbard, Joe Williams, Ricky Betz, Steve Miller, Jason Smith and John Glushick to name a few. These were true ballplayers — they weren't looking for a party, they were looking for *baseball*.

So what do I hope to see in the future? That's simple — more people, young and old, enjoying the game that I love, realizing that baseball *is* the party....

A PERSONAL NOTE

I have to first thank Ted for believing in me way back when. It would have been so easy for him to turn his back on me. He didn't, however. He is truly a great man.

I didn't want to get into all this again (the first time was enough) but now I'm glad I did. We took a picture of me swinging left-handed for the cover. I did it for the sake of dreaming. Ted has dreamed and I have too. Have you ever dreamed? I mean, have you really gone after something — hook, line and sinker — heart, mind and soul? If it's hitting a baseball, I know this book can help.

In closing I'll leave you with the words to a song I wrote. It is featured in the instructional video: "Hitting the Ted Williams Way" (Part One). Good luck and "Get a Good Pitch to Hit!"

FIG 10-14. *In* Disciple of a Master, *I claimed that dreaming — the constant pursuit of a distant desire — was the only stage for an individual's greatest effort. The Ted Williams League is a dream come true.*

Baseball's Where I Begin

Years ago, when I was oh so young.

I found you the place for all my fun.

Days at the playground or right out in the street,

Baseball made life complete—Baseball made life complete.

A black taped ball, on asphalt pictured green,

A broken bat with wood screws still can dream.

Dad bought me my first glove,

My young fist broke it in.

Baseball's where I begin—Baseball's where I begin.

Fresh cut grass, on a Boston night in June.

Rounding the bases, on a pitch you've played a tune.

If you're not with me, this might not be for you.

Baseball's my thing to do.

Now that I'm older and the knees aren't quite the same.

I know for certain, how much I've loved this game.

Cause all it taught me, I still use every day.

Baseball's the game to play—Baseball's the game to play.

FIG 10-15. *If it doesn't all work out the way you had planned... make sure you're able to say that you gave it your best.*

NOTES

NOTES

NOTES

NOTES

NOTES

NOTES